RIGHT THROUGH THE PACK

by ROBERT DARVAS
and NORMAN de V. HART
Assisted by Dr. Paul Stern

Published by
Devyn Press, Inc.
Louisville, Kentucky 40241

First published in 1947 by
Stuyvesant House, New York

Drawings by Stanley Meltzoff.

Printed in the United States of America.

Devyn Press, Inc.
3600 Chamberlain Lane, Suite 230
Louisville, KY 40241
1-800-274-2221

ISBN 0-910791-69-4

INTRODUCTION

ELY CULBERTSON

Introductions, in my opinion, are like after-dinner speeches; both should be short.

So I shall not distract or bore the reader with a dissertation on Contract Bridge in general, or the superiority of this book in particular to so many of the other books on the market.

In simple fairness and honesty, however, I must pay tribute to this book. It is exceptional. First and foremost it contains many beautiful bridge hands. Second, those hands are presented in a way that is, so far as I know, unique, and which, more important, is highly entertaining. Even the most devout bridge addict must yawn as he plows through the ponderous explanations and analyses to be found in so many tomes; but here, the sprightly and clever dialogue, and the basic assumption that the reader is not a moron, form the happiest possible combination.

I must confess that when I was first told about the general concept of this book, in which each card of the pack told its own story, I was not enthusiastic. Indeed, it was as much on my earnest advice as for any other reason that the American publishers decided to dispense with the subtitle adorning the English editions, namely, "A Bridge Fantasy." Americans, I argued, are not strong for fantasy in any form, and certainly not in bridge. We may be a sentimental people, but at the same time we're realistic, and if that be paradox, make the most of it.

But when I had read this book, I knew that I had been partly wrong. There was nothing "too cute" about it! Norman de V. Hart, who is responsible for the prose that points up Robert Darvas' hands, has done a masterful job. Working in a medium studded with pitfalls, he succeeded admirably in avoiding the faintest suggestion of coyness or presciosity. There is a quaint charm to his writing; where someone else might have been doggedly whimsical, he is shrewd and gay, and above all simple.

So, while still applauding the decision to drop the sub-title, "A Bridge Fantasy," because I see no reason to put the proverbial two strikes on a book's cover, I heartily approve of the American publishers' decision to retain the original form throughout all the pages. I understand that several conferences were held to thresh out whether or not to Americanize the English phrasing, and it was finally agreed that whatever might be gained by this "translation," much more would be lost. Thus, you will find the word "Knave" instead of jack used in almost every case because the flavor of the English term matches the flavor of the text so much better. Also, pure British slang and more formal phrases have been let alone, on the good theory that American readers, and particularly American bridge players, can't be baffled so easily.

There is one point on which I should like to caution all readers. You must bear in mind that this is a book presenting cases of magnificent *play*. It is not a text book;

and most definitely it does not purport to be a guide to proper bidding. In many of the deals—*very* many!—the accompanying bidding could not be justified by the world's greatest optimist. Take my advice—forget that! Darvas had to get his declarers to contracts that would demand superlative play; as a fellow writer who has often encountered the same dilemma, I can sympathize with him and therefore forgive him freely when he makes South bid, say, five diamonds on a hand that might possibly be worth a three-diamond bid. And anyway, if we always bid correctly and conservatively, we wouldn't have to be brilliant in the play—we could simply "sit in the rocking chair and pull cards" to make our contracts.

One more salient fact must be mentioned. Quite aside from the pleasure you are going to find in this book—I guarantee that pleasure!—when you finish it you will have become, quite painlessly, a better bridge player!

FOREWORD

BY DR. PAUL STERN

My friends, Robert Darvas and Norman de V. Hart, have asked me to write a foreword to explain how this little bridge fantasy has come to be written by two men who have never met. I rather think they want me publicly to shoulder the responsibility, which indeed is mine.

Robert Darvas is a Hungarian famous for his extraordinary gift of discovering the unusual features of bridge hands —the beautiful, the queer, the exciting and even the comical. If a hand worth acquiring crops up in a rubber at some club or during an unpublicised local tournament, it somehow comes to the knowledge of Robert Darvas.

Throughout the war Darvas lived in Budapest, and collected a number of hands from play. Had communication with the outside world still existed, or had the Hungarian press continued to provide an outlet, most of these would have appeared singly in newspaper bridge columns and bridge magazines throughout the world. As it was Darvas could do nothing with his treasures but hide them in his desk.

When the war ended, he got in touch with me, and told me about his now sizable collection and about his idea of selecting from it fifty-two hands, one for every card in the pack. We agreed that the best way of "putting this over" was to compile a book. Darvas sent me the hands and the stories told by each card in turn, with that card as more or less the key card of the tale.

I could not fail to appreciate the unique quality and extraordinary variety of the hands. Most of the stories, too, appealed to me. But I realised they would need drastic transformation to adapt them to the taste and humour of the English speaking world. Mere translation would not suffice.

To whom in England should I turn for help? At once I remembered Norman Hart's exquisite *"Bridge Player's Bedside Book."* He had, moreover, been collaborating with me in the writing of the new textbook on the Vienna System. I explained Darvas's ideas to him. His only reaction was: "Never again will I write a bridge book." I understood, and said nothing to try to make him change his mind. But I sent him Darvas's manuscript.

A few days later Hart rang me up on the telephone. He was full of delight over the hands and of enthusiasm for Darvas's general notion of each card of the pack coming to life and telling a story. He added the suggestion of creating a fairy world of the cards and having them tell their stories at one time and place, thus linking the tales into a connected whole. Also he agreed with me that many of the stories were not suited to the taste of the English-speaking public, and that different ones would have to be written.

Darvas agreed to Hart's suggestions and that he should have a free hand in fashioning the book, and Hart set to work. Several of the stories had to be abandoned because some of the hands had found their way into the world press. Darvas at once produced other hands to take their place, and by December, 1946, our choice was complete. Five months later the first set of galley proofs was lying on my desk.

That is the story of the book. I take pride in having brought together these two stars in the firmament of bridge writers. I hope that after you have read the book you will find my pride pardonable.

October, 1947
London, England

SPADES

HEARTS

DIAMONDS

CLUBS

RIGHT THROUGH
THE PACK

I AM NOT LEARNED IN FOLK-LORE, AND NEVER BEFORE HAD had any ground for thinking I possessed the strange powers of sight and hearing enjoyed by the fey. More than that, I venture to say the most unlikely hour and place one would look to meet any of the Little People would be when the silver-grey light of a summer dawn was seeping past the edges of drawn blinds to vie uncertainly with shaded lamps in the smoke-hazy air of a bridge club.

I suppose it can be fairly argued, however, that, granted the replacement of wooded sward by green baize cloth, the hour of orthodox pixies and leprechauns and elves

1

just had to out-double-summer time by dawn itself, seeing that card-play does not cease upon the midnight air—no, not by any means. And it would seem, too, there are as many kinds of Little People as there is diversity of human activities. Of ancient times and bucolic life those versed in such matters may speak; but I, a modern, content myself with observing that if we must have aeroplanes, then are we bound to have gremlins. Let me add that now when millions all over the world play bridge, it is equally inevitable there should be a race of Wee Folk created by the thought we humans concentrate so hotly on the pasteboard slips we hold hour after hour in our hands.

You perceive I am trying to rationalise a little the strange adventure that befell me that summer dawn in the deserted bridge room of my thoroughly prosaic club, lest you account it nothing but a dream. I deny that—with all the fierceness of one who fears it might even be so. For I prefer to think that what happened to me did so happen. I must think that, or else I, whose pride is my cold-blooded powers of card-analysis, and whose imagination has always been limited to such matters as trying to foretell which way to finesse, must most distastefully regard myself as a queer and whimsical fellow whose dreams can bring forth a new tribe—nay, four new tribes—of charming Little People, the which, in my waking hours, I know as nothing more than painted and printed aces, court cards, and x's.

But you shall judge for yourselves.

It had been for me a day and night of bridge. I had written a bridge article in the morning; played rubber bridge all the afternoon; and in the evening my team had played a practice match till after midnight. That over, and the visiting team speeded on their way with a farewell glass, we had sat in committee on our gains and losses till one by one my team-mates stole away to answer the call of sleep, leaving the card room empty save for a single solitary figure. I found myself strangely wide awake, and so decided before adjourning the committee of one to give it for consideration from the afternoon's rubber bridge a contract over which I had failed, but which I felt convinced there was a way of making.

I spread the four hands on the table, and set myself to analysis. I remember I was peering hard at the Eight of Diamonds, wondering if I could use it to produce a double squeeze, when suddenly it rose upright, standing on two sturdy little feet, and said, in a small, clear, metallic voice:

"Don't worry about it any longer, Master Robert. It can't be made, even double dummy."

The curious thing is I was not astonished—not then. No, not even when the other fifty-one cards likewise rose upright and a shrill chorus of greetings beat about my ears. All I could distinguish in the tiny clamour was that they all knew me and saluted me in respectful and friendly fashion as "Master Robert."

But though I felt no surprise, I did feel embarrassed. For I did not know how to conduct myself in the presence of so many Royalties. They were only eight out of fifty-two, with four courtiers, in the shape of the handsomely dressed Knaves, but somehow they stood out from the rest so regally in their fine robes and jewelled crowns that I, a mere commoner, was suitably overawed.

3

Then I noticed something quite ridiculous. Two of the cards were standing on their heads, with their feet waving helplessly in the air. I hurriedly picked them up, and set them gently on their feet. They were the Seven of Hearts and the Seven of Clubs.

They thanked me gratefully, and then the Club Seven said:

"You are thoughtful as well as observant, Master Robert. We Sevens are the only inhabitants of the Pack who are not the same either way up."

I looked hastily to see how the Sevens of Diamonds and Spades were situated, and was relieved to find I had happened to place them right way up. The Seven of Hearts joined in:

"We Sevens are proud of our distinction, but if players only knew how we hate being held upside down! Even you, Master Robert, who we well know have a life-long love for all of us in the Pack, sometimes fail us Sevens in this way."

I said how sorry I was, and promised to take more care in future. Then, my self-confidence restored by this incident, I turned to the King and Queen of Hearts, who stood fondly arm-in-arm a little in front of the rest.

"May it please your Most Gracious Majesties," I began when the Queen interrupted me in a rather distressed voice:

"Oh Master Robert, please don't use such formalities. It will do quite well if you just say 'Sir' and 'Mam' when you talk to us. There was a time when the Kings and Queens of the Pack were always addressed ceremoniously; but that was in the early days of bridge, when everyone thought we and the Aces were all that mattered in a hand. But these are democratic days, and we high personages have been taught by master players that our might is little if it is not given the supporting strength that comes from the lesser People of the Pack. True, we Royal Ones are specially counted for defence; but what is that compared with the attacking strength of six or seven of our own suit behind us?"

"Yes," her King broke in, "we have learned our lesson. Too often have we known some witless player with 4-3-3-3 distribution to think to himself: 'Five-and-a-half honour tricks. Grand! I'll open with Two Clubs,' and seen what dreadful things can befall. To-day we know better. We know that a singleton Deuce is often as good as I or any other King, and that a worthless-seeming doubleton may be as valuable even as my sweet lady here." And he looked lovingly at the Queen, who smiled with pleasure, while continuing to gaze straight in front of her.

The King of Clubs strode forward at this point.

"My Heart brother is quite right," he said, a little morosely. "Why, now-a-days you see players counting industriously as soon as they look at a hand—so much for each void or singleton, so much for suit lengths, and so much for us and our courtiers and Prime Ministers—whom you humans call Knaves and Aces. In short, we Kings and Queens to-day are valued on the same basis as lesser folk, and have to justify ourselves exactly as if we were made of the same stuff as they.

"So you are," called out the Five of Spades, with a sort of jovial viciousness. "You've a few more colours than we others, and a bit more printer's ink goes to your making;

5

but none of you can take more than one trick, and we others often do as much."

"That's all you know," rejoined the Ace of Spades, a thickset, beetle-browed, fierce-looking fellow. "Of course none of us can take more than one trick; but you would never do even that if it wasn't for the promoting power we Honours exercise to give you and your kind the ability to take any sort of trick."

"What about the number of times I and many of my like have ruffed you?" yelled the Three of Diamonds.

There followed a hubub of shouts and counter-shouts, accusations and retorts. But somehow it seemed as though it was all an old and unsettled quarrel that by now had lost much of its original enmity and become pretence and habit. Quiet was at once restored when I intervened to calm them. The novelty of talking to me evidently meant more to them than an ancient and worn-out feud. The Little People looked warningly at each other, and then apologised gracefully to me.

"But tell me something," I said. "The King of Hearts spoke just now of what a player thought to himself. Do you mean to say you People of the Pack"—they all looked pleased at that form of address, and I was glad I had made a mental note of it when the Heart Queen was speaking— "know what players think? Can you really read their minds?"

"Indubitably we can," said the Knave of Spades, who had only one eye. This had given him an inferiority complex, for which he sought compensation in a rather pedantic and pompous way of speaking. "Indubitably." He savoured the word as he repeated it, and then went on: "To be precise, directly a player starts arranging his hand, we have a fair idea of his abilities, if any. I do not refer to the abominable practice of placing us so that the figures and suit symbols in our top left-hand corners and even those in our bottom right-hand corners are scarcely visible. That imparts to us a malaise almost as disturbing as if we were all inverted Sevens."

There were murmurs of assent, and the Queen of Diamonds said: "Besides, it is very unkind to the poor kibitzer."

"But even more upsetting for the poor dear opponent who likes a peep," mocked the Knave of Clubs, with a chuckle.

"Nor do I refer," went on the Knave of Spades, just as though there had been no interruption, "to the way some players hold us in both hands and move us continually back and forth from one hand to the other in restless, febrile review. For even among master players these and other queer, if less annoying, habits have occasionally been observed. What I mean is something less obvious than mannerisms—the very feel of the player's fingers and the way he looks at us. At once, if he is a mediocrity, we can tell he is not seeing the reality and true meaning of us and of the manner in which we are combined in his hand. As the bidding proceeds, we are soon confirmed in our estimate of him, for we can sense how cloudy and imprecise is his mind. Sometimes we can scarce perceive through the cloudiness what in fact he is thinking, though often we are uncomfortably aware that his thoughts are all on wrong lines, and that he has either failed to heed or misconstrued the significance of the other players' bidding. Thus is it that when the final contract is reached, he is generally left quite uncertain whether it be right or wrong, doubtful or a practical certainty. As with bidding, so too with playing. More often than not he does not know what he is doing, and that is very boring for us because we know so much more than he does. Similarly when a master holds us, we soon become aware of that piece of good fortune which befalls us all too seldom. There is no cloudiness in a master's mind; and we look with joy into its crystal-like clarity and watch his thoughts marshalling themselves in disciplined forms—inferring, calculating, observing, interpreting, judging. Then we are glad, and rejoice we were born into that Pack. For then is it that we often learn something we did not know before. To be badly played is horrible to us; but to be played in a way even we could not foresee, as a master sometimes does, is for us the greatest happiness to which we can attain."

"So you can see into our minds," I said. "I had no idea that whenever I pick up a hand I have a jury of thirteen trying me."

"More than that," interposed the Queen of Clubs, a fragile, sensitive-looking little brunette. "We don't only see into your minds; we see into your hearts as well. We know what you are feeling—hopes and fears, your elation at winning and whether you are losing more than you can afford. And we don't all hate and despise bad players, as the Knave of Spades does. Some of us have the decency to be sorry for them and try to help them, especially those who honestly do their best and are not puffed up with vanity."

"But how is it you People of the Pack can know our thoughts and feelings?" I asked.

The Three of Spades answered.

"We see your thoughts by looking into your brain through your eyes as they rest on us spread out in your hand."

"That I can believe," I replied; "but how do you know about our emotions?"

This time the reply came from the Eight of Diamonds, who had started the whole affair by rising and speaking to me.

"Do you imagine," he asked, "that you can hold us in your hand, with the warmth of your flesh vitalising us and with your pulse faintly perceptible to us in your fingers, and not communicate your feelings to us? For the time being each Group of Thirteen dealt to you becomes part of you and of your life. Have you not often felt that for the moment you and that Group of Thirteen are one and indivisible? So too do we feel. The blood that courses through your veins seems to pass through us, and your emotions are not merely known to us, but often become as our own. Generally these emotions are concentrated on the bidding and the play, on the rubber or the match. But sometimes, as the Queen of Clubs has said, these feelings have a somewhat wider range, and give us a glimpse of your existence as persons. We can thus spot the habitual optimist and the habitual pessimist, the frivolous individual and the serious-minded, the sadist and the masochist. And then once in a long while something happens which enables us to see farther still. On these rare occasions we are able to perceive, as in a dim mirror, a faint image of human life beyond the game and the play and the bridge club itself—in the great world where we of the Pack have no part. I remember once—"

A MIRACULOUS GRAND SLAM

(The Tale of the Eight of Diamonds)

IT WAS A PARTNERSHIP EVENING AT THE CLUB, AND THERE was one pair in whom I found myself taking a strong interest. They were a man and a girl, she in the early twenties and he a few years older. He was intelligent and had character, and I judged him a trustworthy fellow whose love would be any woman's good fortune. I mention this because I had not been dealt to him more than two or three times before I knew that for him the whole meaning of life was centred on that girl.

She, too, had intelligence and character, and with them charm and gaiety; but it did not take long for me to realise that there was one thing she could not do—and that was to play bridge. You humans are said each to have, even the best of you, some little spot of madness. Julie's tiny share of insanity was to want to play bridge well and successfully when the pity was she just had no ability that way, though I've no doubt she was quite an efficient young person away from the card table.

Johnny, who was a first-rate player, had naturally done his best to help her in her ambition by teaching her the game. The result was she knew all the rules and maxims of good play—I've said she was intelligent—but was quite unable to apply them.

However, I was not much interested in how she played. Directly I learned Johnny loved her, I was all agog to find out whether she loved him. The next time I was dealt to her I concentrated on interpreting the throbs of her heart in the soft tips of her slender fingers.

She liked Johnny a lot, it seemed, and loved him quite a little. But with you humans, I am given to understand, there is always one who kisses and one who is kissed. She was the kissed one. May-be she was a trifle cold in her nature. May-be she was somewhat scared by the strength of Johnny's feeling for her. May-be her man had not yet

12

crossed her path. Whatever the reason, she wasn't sure she wanted to marry Johnny. But also she wasn't sure she didn't. Just at that moment Julie, I sensed, was ready to be swayed either way.

And Johnny had decided to propose marriage to her that night when he took her home after their evening of bridge. He felt that after several hours of successful partnership—he was determined to make it that—she would not view unfavourably turning it into a wider and more permanent affair.

Did he make a successful partnership that night? Yes and no. Julie's greatest failing at the game was her inordinate fondness for Forcing Bids. She took a delight in seeing the wheels go round, and she enjoyed the mild sensation a Forcing Bid always creates. Johnny knew this, and feared her Forcing Bids like the devil. The difficulty was that sometimes, of course, they were justified. Then, if he held back and made discouraging responses, a slam would be missed—to Julie's indignant disappointment.

Well, that night they held goodish cards most of the time, and towards the end of the session were modest winners. Julie wanted more than that. Twice she forced, and twice Johnny held back fearfully, and twice a slam was missed. He apologised and took all the blame—rightly, for her Forces happened to be thoroughly sound. Then he held a really good hand, and bid and made a Small Slam. Julie's delight was tinged with a touch of jealousy that her two big hands had gone astray.

Came the last rubber of the evening, and each side won a game. Julie was now out for blood, if there was the slightest sign of it being about. And then Johnny, sitting South let us say, dealt me to himself thus:

♠ A 7 4
♡ A J 9 3
◇ K 8 4 2
♣ K 3

Johnny bid a Heart. From her face I could see that Julie rather fancied her hand. It was:

♠ 6 5 3
♡ K 4 2
◇ A J
♣ A 9 5 4 2

She bid Two Clubs. On hearing Two No-Trumps from Johnny, Julie, determined on a glorious finish to the evening, jumped straight to Blackwood's Four No-Trumps. Johnny admitted having two Aces by responding with Five Hearts, and Julie promptly went to Seven Hearts.

It was not till West led the King of Spades and she had to put her hand on the table, that doubts began to ruffle her serenity.

"I think I've rather overbid this collection," she remarked, with a tremulous gaiety.

I felt Johnny draw in his breath sharply as dummy went down; but he recovered himself quickly.

"No," he said, bravely, "It's all right, Julie. Perhaps the Small Slam *would* have been safer . . ."

"We haven't had a Grand Slam all evening," she excused herself; "and I did so want just one. But my Club suit does look rather moth-eaten spread out on the table. I wish it were a wee bit more solid." Her laugh was a trifle unnatural.

He detected a hint of tears in it, and told her heroically: "Don't you worry, Old Thing. You bid the hand beautifully. Now it's up to me." And he set himself to examine the situation.

I was more moved than I can say. It seemed so hopeless and I could see his thoughts so clearly through his troubled eyes. At first they were not analytical.

"If I can land this ridiculous slam," he told himself, "she'll be terribly pleased. I somehow feel it'll just make the difference when I tell her what I'm going to to-night. It's queer, but I believe that if I fail at this, I shall fail with her afterwards. I've just *got* to make the damned contract. But how? Suppose luck is completely with me. Is there a possible distribution of opponents' hands that will give me a chance? Can anything be done with that miserable Club suit?

"Let me see. Suppose everything breaks right and all finesses come off. Then I can make four Club tricks by ruffing the third round—that's five tricks—and three trump tricks, three Diamonds, and a Spade. Twelve tricks. Where's the thirteenth to come from? What about ruffing a Diamond in dummy? Ah-ha! perhaps that will work.

15

```
♠ 6 5 3
♡ K 4 2
♢ A J
♣ A 9 5 4 2

        N
    W       E
        S

♠ A 7 4
♡ A J 9 3
♢ K 8 4 2
♣ K 3
```

"Let's see. Take the first trick with the Ace of Spades. Then finesse the Knave of Diamonds. A low Heart from dummy, double-finessing the Nine. Over to the Diamond Ace. Another low Heart, finessing the Knave. Cash Diamond King, discarding one of dummy's Spades. Ruff a Diamond in dummy with the King. Return to my hand with the King of Clubs. Draw last trump with Ace. Play Ace of Clubs, and ruff a small Club. Clubs are now good. But, damn it, there's no entry to dummy to cash them. Oh, curse! That won't work. What am I to do? It can't be made—it simply can't."

I was feeling distraught myself, and gazed pityingly at him, trying to catch his eye. At last I succeeded, and I gave him a sympathetic smile which I tried to make encouraging as well, for I had a feeling that I was the key to the solution of his problem. He looked at me, and I saw hope lighten the despair in his mind.

"Gosh!" he said. "Could that be possible? Can I set up the Eight of Diamonds without ruffing? Then I could discard two Spades from Dummy on the King and Eight of Diamonds. Yes, it might be done—but only if West has Queen-Ten-Nine of Diamonds and just two trumps, the Queen and Ten. In that case there should be an end-play. It's absolutely the only hope. So here goes!"

And he began to play. Here is the complete deal:

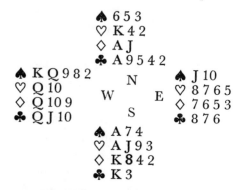

```
              ♠ 6 5 3
              ♡ K 4 2
              ◇ A J
              ♣ A 9 5 4 2
♠ K Q 9 8 2        N        ♠ J 10
♡ Q 10                      ♡ 8 7 6 5
◇ Q 10 9      W      E      ◇ 7 6 5 3
♣ Q J 10           S        ♣ 8 7 6
              ♠ A 7 4
              ♡ A J 9 3
              ◇ K 8 4 2
              ♣ K 3
```

Johnny made the first trick with the Ace of Spades; finessed the Knave of Diamonds, West playing the Nine; and laid down the Diamond Ace, dropping West's Ten. The King and Ace of Hearts dropped West's Ten and Queen, and then the Diamond King and I were played, two of dummy's Spades being discarded on us. Johnny now ruffed the Four of Spades in dummy, and returned to his hand with the King of Clubs. The Knave of Hearts was played and then the position was:

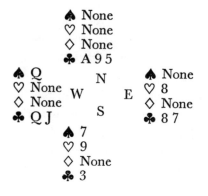

```
              ♠ None
              ♡ None
              ◇ None
              ♣ A 9 5
♠ Q               N        ♠ None
♡ None                     ♡ 8
◇ None        W      E      ◇ None
♣ Q J              S        ♣ 8 7
              ♠ 7
              ♡ 9
              ◇ None
              ♣ 3
```

Johnny led the Nine of Hearts, and West was squeezed. If he threw a Club, he would make dummy's Nine of Clubs good. So he gave up his Spade, faintly hoping his partner might have the thirteenth of the suit. Johnny's Seven of Spades and dummy's Ace of Clubs took the last two tricks.

He looked across at Julie, and said, triumphantly:

"Made it!"

Julie who had watched the play at first anxiously, but afterwards, as Johnny gathered in trick after trick, with relief and pleasure, now said in a voice of placid content:

"It was lucky the Diamond finesse came off. I know it was wrong of me to bid the Grand Slam on a finesse; but otherwise it was all right, just as you said. And not so difficult to make after all."

*   *   *

The Little People laughed appreciatively; and then the Queen of Spades asked:

"Did all end happily ever after?"

The Eight of Diamonds nodded.

"I hope so," he said. "I never saw Julie again—they were both just visitors—but Johnny came into the club a few days later to say good-bye, and I heard several of the members congratulating him. So I think that Grand Slam served a good purpose."

"May-be and may-be not," put in the Knave of Clubs, a swash-buckling yet withal a foxy-looking fellow. "Johnny is welcome to his Julie for all I care. I don't believe in this pandering to the conceit of women for their favours. Treat 'em rough, and make 'em like it, is my motto. Apart from

the revolting sentimentality Diamond Eight has been mush-
ing us up in, what does it all amount to but the story of a
bad contract—so fantastically bad that the odds against
finding the only distribution against it on which it could
be made must be about 500,000 to one. I don't blame anyone for getting into a bad contract. That comes the way of
every player once in a while. But to suit my taste, let it be
a contract—when it has to be a bad one—that gives a player some chance for roguery and deceit. What more exquisite thrill can a bridge player experience than to make a
quite impossible contract by tricking his opponents and
making 'em look a complete pair of fools! What say you,
Master Robert? Listen, and I'll tell you of just such a case,
in which I, in the hand of a brilliant rascal to whom I take
off my hat whenever I think of that adventure, was able to
perform the most crafty piece of knavishness of my whole
career—"

THE COMEDY OF A RUSE

(*The Tale of the Knave of Clubs*)

THE FIRST TIME THOSE LEAN, BROWN YOUNG FINGERS
picked me up off the table, and I felt those dare-devil blue
eyes looking at me, I knew there would be little dullness for
me that evening. When the Pack is cut and dealt at an
R.A.F. fighter station, there is one thing sure—play won't
be hampered by the phobias and inhibitions that haunt
bridge clubs. But while my fine young rascal played as live-

ly a game as the rest of them, it did not take me long to realise he had a flair that seldom led him astray; and that when it did, he had at his call an impudent ingenuity which frequently saved him from seemingly inevitable disaster. At times one could almost believe he deliberately got himself into a hole for the sheer fun of seeing if he could get out of it.

Presently I was in his hand again, thus:

♠ Q 8
♡ K 10 7 3
◇ K 10 9 5 4 2
♣ 4

```
        N
   W         E
        S
```

♠ 9 6 2
♡ A 6
◇ Q J 8 6 3
♣ A K J

He opened the bidding with One Diamond, and received the reply of Three Diamonds. Quite nonchalantly, he bid Three No-Trumps, and the Group Captain on his left led a small Club. I alone noticed the wide blue eyes narrow slightly when dummy went down and he saw that the Spade suit was open to the winds.

His fore-finger flicked dummy's Club onto the trick.

Then when the Squadron Leader on his right played the Club Queen, he dropped me without a flicker of hesitation. The Squadron Leader continued the suit eagerly at the sight of me, and with careful carelessness my clever young master took the trick with the Ace. Now he led a Diamond, and the Group Captain's Ace pounced on the trick. Obviously, the Club suit was his to run, and run it he would. Triumphantly he led a Club.

I shan't ever forget his look of horrified astonishment when Blue Eyes quietly took the trick with the King, and forthwith made his contract with five Diamonds, two Hearts, and two Clubs.

With an air of elaborate innocence, he then remarked: "That was a bit of luck. Do you know, if it had occurred to one of you two types to play Spades, I should have had it?"

Then the Group Captain and Squadron Leader broke their stupefied silence. What they said to each other was couched in words known only to airmen. But I gathered that each thought the other should have switched to Spades, and each felt the other should have known Blue Eyes better than to trust the evidence of his play. They didn't, as far as I could judge, reach any very satisfactory conclusion.

The only contribution made by the boy who had been dummy, was this cryptic remark to Blue Eyes:

"I give you a gong for that piece of play."

Then the Group Captain said something I could understand. He asked Blue Eyes:

"Why in Hades did you bid No-Trumps without any Spades?"

23

With lifted eyebrows, that gentleman replied:

"Because there's no game in Diamonds—unless, of course, your aversion to leading Spades is chronic."

That remark might have led to a riot in a bridge club. But the Group Captain only laughed. They are like that in the R.A.F.

*　　*　　*

"An excellent example of an opportunity seized and exploited," said the Ace of Diamonds.

"There speaks the politician," remarked the Four of Clubs. Then for my benefit he explained:

"You see, Master Robert, the Aces, being the only citizens of the Pack more powerful than the Kings, are our Prime Ministers—one for each of the four tribes. And what is a Prime Minister but a particularly successful politician?"

"Occasionally he is a statesman," I murmured.

"Yes," said the Seven of Clubs. "The ancient Greeks had a proverb: First acquire wealth; then practice virtue. With Prime Ministers it has generally been a case of: First play politics successfully; then practice statesmanship."

The Eight of Hearts here became explanatory.

"You will find the Club tribe pert and self-assertive and cynical, Master Robert, and may wonder why. It's because as the lowest of the four tribes, they have built themselves up a superiority complex in self-defence."

There was indignant outcry from the Clubs, but the rest of the Pack merely laughed indulgently. Then the Two of Clubs spoke in a sad, complaining little voice:

"I have no feeling of superiority. The clever trick of the young airman was legitimate, and the Knave of our tribe

24

was entitled to be proud of the part he played. But as for me, something lately happened which has besmirched and disgraced me forever. That it should have befallen the weakest and smallest inhabitant of the Pack is indeed hard. All I have is my honesty and respectability. To take these from me—"

"Stop moaning," interrupted the King of Clubs, "and tell us what this terrible thing was."

"Very good, Your Majesty," said the Club Deuce, bowing low before his Monarch. "I will."

The poor little chap wiped his eyes, which had filled with tears of self-pity; straightened himself importantly when he realised all ears were turned curiously towards him; and began—

A FAT MAN'S VILLAINY

(*The Tale of the Two of Clubs*)

I AM ABLE TO TAKE LITTLE PART IN THE GREAT BATTLE FOR tricks that goes on over my head. True, I can perform vital duties, such as providing an entry to the hand opposite or enabling a player to exit at the right moment. I may even make a trick in my own right as thirteenth of the tribe. But these are rare and prized occasions. Then sometimes my tribe are trumps, and I get a chance to ruff a high member of another tribe—once in a while even a Royal Personage or a Prime Minister. Mainly, however, my work is rather menial, such as signalling discouragement or playing the minor role in an encouraging peter.

Nevertheless, taking one thing with another, I had come to feel I was a useful enough citizen of the Pack, and had fortified my lowly, hard-working life with a little harmless self-esteem. And then—

(The poor little Deuce shook his head mournfully and sighed before he went on).

It was a few days ago, during that heat-wave which, you remember, made us all go limp and sticky in the players' damp hands. About the middle of the afternoon I found myself held clammily in the large fat hand of a large fat man, to whom I took an instant dislike. His eyes were small and close together. His face, round and loosely fleshy, wore a continuous smile of bonhomie I instinctively distrusted. His several chins wobbled as he talked and laughed—he laughed a good deal and as a habit—and his neck at the back was a purple bulge. The heat obviously caused him much discomfort.

I, too, felt discomfort—more at the touch of his thick, sweaty fingers than from the heat. I looked around for distraction, and perceived that the deal was:

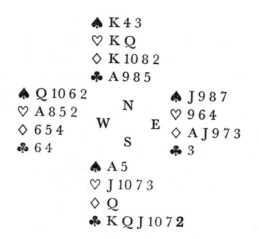

♠ K 4 3
♥ K Q
♦ K 10 8 2
♣ A 9 8 5

♠ Q 10 6 2   ♠ J 9 8 7
♥ A 8 5 2   N   ♥ 9 6 4
♦ 6 5 4 W   E ♦ A J 9 7 3
♣ 6 4   S   ♣ 3

♠ A 5
♥ J 10 7 3
♦ Q
♣ K Q J 10 7 2

The fat man, sitting South, opened with One Club, and after a couple of rounds of bidding went to Six Clubs. When dummy was tabled, I was glad to see there were two Aces for opponents to make. But my hated fat man showed no sign of being worried. Why not? I wondered. Alas! I was soon to know.

West led the Ace of Hearts, and then shifted to the Deuce of Spades, which Fat Man took in his hand with the Ace. He drew trumps in two rounds with the King and Queen, and entered dummy with a Heart. Then came the crucial moment.

Leaning his large bulk across the table, he carefully picked out dummy's Eight of Diamonds at the lead, and then leaned heavily back in his chair panting with the heat. East fingered his Ace of Diamonds, and hesitated. While he hesitated, Fat Man—I shudder as I recall it—seized me in his right hand, and fanned his great hot, moist face with me. The still hesitant East could not but perceive that it was a low trump waving back and forth, and that decided him into thinking South must be devoid of Diamonds, and that I, poor innocent, was being held in readiness to ruff his Ace.

He played a small Diamond to the trick. Whereupon Fat Man replaced me in his hand, and played the Diamond Queen. The slam was thus made. East said no word. How could he? He himself was not guiltless. Nor could he even be sure Fat Man had indeed intended to trap him.

But I was sure. I saw the gleam of villainy in Fat Man's eyes as he brought shame and disgrace into my honourable, if unhonoured, life.

* * *

Again the heart-broken Deuce broke into tears. I could not but find some humour in the tale he had told ; but I quickly straightened my face when I saw how shocked the Wee Folk were, as they crowded round the weeping little Club, seeking to console him with words and friendly caresses. They were still engaged in this kindly fashion when the King of Diamonds, separating himself from the rest, stepped towards me, and said:

"You may wonder, Master Robert, that we see nothing even faintly funny in that episode. I know you humans, while thinking all sharp practice utterly reprehensible, can be amused at some clever piece of trickery even in the moment of denouncing it. Especially is this so when the person tricked had himself no right to take advantage of the information proffered, and acted on it entirely at his own risk if it proved false. But with us it is different. We people of the

Pack know our very existence depends on the game being kept clean and straight. For if honourable men and women were compelled to abandon the game, we People of the Pack, whose supernatural life comes from the human thoughts of those who love the game for the game's sake, would sink back into the Nothingness from which we came."

By this time the Two of Clubs appeared to have recovered himself sufficiently, for the Wee Folk began to return to hear what the Diamond King and I were talking about. The Knave of Spades now spoke in his rather pedantic way:

"The King of Diamonds is quite right, and I am glad he has acquainted you, Master Robert, with the very high Code of Ethics for which we People of the Pack stand. For you might, perchance, have misinterpreted what my cousin, the Knave of Clubs, said about the way we Knaves rejoice at roguery and trickery. Such feats must always remain strictly within the Laws. Here is an example—"

"But it is nonsense," broke in the Five of Hearts, "for these Knaves to talk as if they had a monopoly of appreciation for honest and legitimate ruses and false trails. Let me tell you, Master Robert, of one such exploit in which I was concerned a short while ago."

"Not so," the Knave of Spades interrupted, heatedly. "I had started to tell Master Robert an adventure of mine."

"You shall both tell your tales," I soothed them; "but first the Knave, who did in fact begin."

"Mine is not long," said the mollified Spade; "yet I think you will find it worth a hearing, Master Robert. Then I will gladly listen in my turn to the Five of Hearts."

31

A FATAL CHANGE OF PLAN

(*The Tale of the Knave of Spades*)

I, TOO, HAVE TO TELL OF A BRILLIANT *ruse de guerre*; BUT, unlike the young airman, the protagonist of my story did not have to make a lightning decision, though at the moment of the crucial play the least flicker of hesitation would have revealed it was a subterfuge. On the occasion in question I found myself dealt to one of those players whom I admire above all others—players who decline to regard any situation as hopeless, and who always seek for ways of evading defeats which most people tamely accept as inevitable. He sat East, and this was the deal and the bidding:

```
                    ♠ A Q 10 8 6
                    ♡ 9 8
                    ◇ Q J 8
                    ♣ Q 4 2
    ♠ 7 3                            ♠ K J 5
    ♡ A J 6 5 3 2        N          ♡ Q 4
    ◇ 6 3           W       E       ◇ K 4 2
    ♣ 10 7 3            S           ♣ J 9 8 6 5
                    ♠ 9 4 2
                    ♡ K 10 7
                    ◇ A 10 9 7 5
                    ♣ A K
```

SOUTH	NORTH
1 ◇	1 ♠
2 ◇	2 ♠
2 N-T	3 N-T
No bid	

West led the Five of Hearts. My man, East, played the Queen; and South took the trick with the King. South perceived that the contract depended on successful finessing, since the opponents had at least four Hearts to make as soon as either of them could obtain the lead. There was a choice of two suits for declarer to play on—Spades and Diamonds. The former lacked both King and Knave, while in the latter only the King was missing. It did not

34

take South long to decide that Diamonds offered the better chance. He therefore led a small Spade from his hand, and played dummy's Ace to the trick, preparatory to finessing Diamonds through East.

But that astute individual had been making good use of the few precious moments of time South's brief planning had given him. He at once realised, from South's rebid of Diamonds, that the position of his Diamond King was hopeless, and that the successful finesse in that suit would give South five tricks and in all probability his contract. He wasted not a second in idle regrets, but straightway sought some means of causing South to go astray. To my admiration and joy, he found it.

When South put up dummy's Ace of Spades, my man instantly dropped his King on it. South's surprise quickly turned into pleasure, for he now saw a way of avoiding what to him was the hazard of the Diamond finesse. Returning to his hand with a Club, he first cashed his other winning Club, and then led the Nine of Spades, and finessed. But I won the trick, and my man returned a Heart. Thus the contract was defeated. East had executed the only manoeuvre that could induce the declarer to abandon his winning plan for one that must lose.

*   *   *

As the somewhat lecturing voice ceased on a note of triumph, there came a low, approving hum from the gathering. I told the Knave of Spades, who was looking anxiously at me, how excellent I thought his narrative. Then the Ten of Diamonds spoke reflectively:

"It's curious how alike and yet different is this defensive trick compared with that of the Fighter Pilot as declarer. Both consist of the spectacular dropping of Court persons to deceive opponents; both had to be put into action as early as the first two rounds. Yet one was designed to induce an opponent to abandon his carefully chosen line of play, while the purpose of the other was at all costs to ensure that opponents should stick to their original plan. I find that distinctly piquant."

The impetuous Five of Hearts burst in boisterously:

"And I find both ruses blatant and violent—what the Diamond Ten more politely calls spectacular. I am glad the Knave of Spades took the floor before me, for the exploit I'm going to tell will gain by contrast. Its key-note is unobtrusiveness, and it had a master mind for its execution. With ordinary players there would have arisen no problem or special difficulty in attack or defence. That is why I choose as title—"

HIDDEN TREASURE

(The Tale of the Five of Hearts)

LOOK WELL AT THESE FOUR HANDS, AND TELL ME IF YOU
do not think it will take a veritable feat of unearthing to
bring treasure to light here.

```
                  ♠ K J 10 4
                  ♡ K 6 3
                  ◇ K 8 4
                  ♣ Q 10 3
    ♠ 8 6 3 2            N           ♠ Q 5
    ♡ J 10 4                         ♡ Q 9 8 5
    ◇ 7 6 5       W         E        ◇ Q J 10 2
    ♣ K 7 5            S             ♣ A 6 4
                  ♠ A 9 7
                  ♡ A 7 2
                  ◇ A 9 3
                  ♣ J 9 8 2
```

South bid a Club, and said One No-Trumps over North's One Spade. North then raised him to Three No-Trumps, and West led the Knave of Hearts. A sound enough contract, and nothing at all striking about the hands, is there? The whole thing seems positively humdrum—the sort of every-day affair one expects to come across half-a-dozen times in any bridge session. Obviously all the declarer has to do is to guess which way to finesse Spades. If he guesses right, he should lose only four tricks; if he guesses wrong, he will be down one.

But then that leaves out of account the circumstance that I and my brothers, the Nine and Eight, and our gracious Queen had been dealt to a brilliant continental international, who, before you humans began your great war, helped to win many championships for his country. No hand is likely to stay ordinary long when he is at the table. See, then, what he made of this one.

A low Heart from dummy was put on West's lead of the Knave, East played the Eight, and South took the trick with his Ace. He led a Club, taken by West's King, and West's lead of the Ten of Hearts drew dummy's King, East playing the Nine. The declarer led Clubs from dummy. East ducked once, and then his Ace made. He cashed the Queen of Hearts, but, although all followed, he just didn't cash me, the thirteenth Heart! Instead he led the Knave of Diamonds, which South's Ace took.

Now South was a good player, too and he duly noted that East had not played me. Therefore, he concluded, it was West who held me. Clearly, he must not allow West to get the lead, for he could afford to lose one more trick to the Spade finesse, if need be; but not two tricks. So he confidently laid down the Ace of Spades, and led a small Spade to dummy, finessing the Knave. East took the trick with his Queen, and then at last quietly cashed me as the trick that defeated the contract.

How does that appeal to you, Master Robert, as a gentle and untheatrical coup? All East did was to play throughout as though he did not possess little me, the Five, until such time as he had persuaded South by these means to let him take a trick with the Queen of Spades. It is one thing to achieve deception by the flamboyant sacrifice of some high personage of the Pack; it is another to entice a wary opponent to his own destruction by concealing what I believe the Americans call a five-spot.

And South must have been a wary opponent, mark you, to have noticed that I had not yet been played. I wonder what would have happened if South had been an indifferent

```
              ♠ K J 10 4
              ♡ K 6 3
              ◇ K 8 4
              ♣ Q 10 3
♠ 8 6 3 2              ♠ Q 5
♡ J 10 4    N         ♡ Q 9 8 5
◇ 7 6 5   W   E       ◇ Q J 10 2
♣ K 7 5     S         ♣ A 6 4
              ♠ A 9 7
              ♡ A 7 2
              ◇ A 9 3
              ♣ J 9 8 2
```

player. Quite possibly he would not have missed me—the small thirteenth of my tribe. In that event he might quite well have decided to finesse into West's hand, and made his contract with an over-trick. In truth, there are some deceptive plays that need for their execution an opponent good enough to be deceived.

*   *   *

Admiring comment rippled across the gathering of tiny beings, and the Knave of Diamonds said:

"One of the best points in the story, I think, is the way that fellow, East, led me and not the Queen of our tribe. To heighten and complete the illusion of not possessing the Five of Hearts by executing what, to the declarer, must have looked for all the world like an entry-creating play to help West get the lead some time so as to cash the thirteenth Heart—that was the crowning touch of an artist."

It was at this point that astonishment overcame me. Till then I had accepted the whole amazing affair as quite natural and ordinary. These queer little persons treated me and themselves and our intercourse as though it was all in the customary way of things, and I had just fallen in with their simple and friendly philosophy. But now, suddenly, realisation was born. I became aware of how unique an adventure was mine, how privileged a mortal was I, who had never imagined it could be my fortune to penetrate beyond the everyday world of the senses.

With new and growing interest I looked more seeingly at the delightful fairy microcosm into which I had been welcomed with a comradeship so charming and at the same time so matter-of-fact.

I perceived that the elfin community of the Pack was composed of living individuals—not cards ; and that their inevitable rectangularity was more an impression than a fact. I perceived, too, how the four orders within the community differed in character. The Spades were swarthy aristocrats, with a touch of hauteur in the air of authority they wore. The Hearts, blonde and plump, bore themselves with a gentle, comfortable sense of security that cultivated sentiment in a measured, bourgeois way. Bright, auburn-haired little sprites were the Diamonds, with sharp, bird-like faces and keen, quick-witted tongues; while the Clubs had flowing black locks and busy brows over dark, piercing eyes, and carried their quaint, gnomish shapes with a bravado at once mischievous and amiable.

I emerged from contemplation of my fifty-two lilliputian hosts and hostesses to hear the King of Diamonds saying:

"I was once concerned in a clever piece of defensive play which, for all that it was what the Five of Hearts scorns as spectacular, passed off quietly enough at the time. But it had a sequel of which you shall hear in my story of—"

A QUARRELSOME SUBALTERN

(*The Tale of the King of Diamonds*)

THE SCENE WAS AN OFFICER'S MESS IN A GARRISON TOWN
some years ago when tanks were still novelties, commandos
and paratroops unheard of, and the only enemy was boredom. A new young officer joined the Mess that night. According to Napoleon, every soldier carries a Marshal's
baton in his knapsack. To my way of thinking that sandy-
haired, quiet-mannered boy carried his baton in his face. As
soon as I felt the firm, confident way he dealt us and picked
us up and looked at us, I knew him as a commander of
men; and when I gazed through his eyes, set wide apart

43

in a rather heavy brow, and saw into his mind, I sensed that time and circumstances were but waiting to make him a commander of armies.

But that was after dinner, when the Colonel, a fine old fellow who kept boredom at bay with his dearly loved half-dozen rubbers of bridge every evening, had called for the card-tables to be set up. I was dealt a few times to another Subaltern, not so young, whose promotion was overdue, and who found bridge alone an insufficient ally against the common enemy. He liked the game well enough, but I soon observed that his irritability was both effect and cause of his rather too frequent signs to the mess orderlies to fill up his glass.

More than that. I learned, in the way we People of the Pack do, that at dinner that first night of his arrival the sandy-haired young Subaltern had somehow won the instant disfavor of his not so young colleague. I think that feeling was the involuntary tribute of mediocrity to character, of dreaded failure to futurity of success. Queerly enough, what particularly annoyed the elder subaltern was that the boy assumed no airs, and showed a sincere and admiring liking for the Colonel, who naturally paid the new arrival some attention with the kindly desire to put him at his ease.

Well, the Colonel had his half-dozen rubbers that night. The two Subalterns both played at his table. Once, when they were partners against the Colonel and the Adjutant, Sandy Hair doubled the Colonel in Three No-Trumps, and the contract was defeated by one trick. The Colonel remarked approvingly:

"Well played, you two!"

And the game went on, with no further comment on the hand than that.

Then, about eleven o'clock, the Colonel, as was his wont, said good-night and retired to his own quarters. Sandy Hair, too, rose and murmured something about thinking it would be a good idea to go and finish his unpacking and hit the hay early, when the other Subaltern, who had been nursing a silent grievance, burst out:

"Just a moment before you go, young fellow. I think you may as well be told now as later that you'll get nowhere in this joint by making up to the Colonel as you've done all night. You'll merely sicken the old boy and get on the wrong side of the rest of us. So you can just chuck it here and now."

Sandy Hair looked dumbfounded at being thus attacked, and stood pale and uncomfortable, looking round the circle of men. For a moment they, too, were taken aback. Then they tried to forestall an open quarrel. Some sought to quieten the angry Subaltern, and others to reassure Sandy Hair. But that young man had quickly regained possession of himself. He sat down at the card table opposite his assailant, and said in quiet, firm tones:

"I just don't get it. What can have made you think I have tried to curry favour with the Colonel. He's been kind and friendly to me as a newcomer, and I've been as polite and pleasant as I could to him. Why not? I think he's a grand old boy. I just don't know what you mean."

"Oh, you don't, don't you?" returned the other heatedly. "What about that time you deliberately doubled the Colonel in Three No-Trumps, when you thought you hadn't a hope of getting him down, and then tried to make sure of giving him his contract by throwing away your high cards? You'd have succeeded, too, if I hadn't seen through your plan and taken the lead and forced you to get him down one. If that isn't making up to him, I'd like to know what you call it."

The boy gave a short chuckle of relief, and a gleam of amusement stole into his troubled eyes as he began to spread out the cards into four hands.

"This is the deal you mean, isn't it?" he asked.

Adjutant
♠ A 4
♡ K 10 4
◇ A 3
♣ Q 10 9 6 5 3

Angry Subaltern
♠ 9 7 3
♡ 9 7 5 2
◇ J 9 7 4 2
♠ 4

N
W E
S

Sandy Hair
♠ J 8 6 5 2
♡ A Q 8
◇ K 10 8
♣ A K

Colonel
♠ K Q 10
♡ J 6 3
◇ Q 6 5
♣ J 8 7 2

"You were West and I was East," Sandy Hair went on. "The Adjutant sat North and the Colonel South. The bidding went:

NORTH	EAST	SOUTH	WEST
1 ♣	Double	No bid	1 ◇
2 ♣	No bid	2 N-T	No bid
3 N-T	Double	No bid	No bid
No bid			

"You led the Four of Diamonds, and after some thought the Colonel put up dummy's Ace. I threw my King under the Ace, and the Colonel played the Five. He then led a Club, which put me in, and I led the Ten of Diamonds, to which—"

"Yes, that's just what I mean," broke in the angry Subaltern. "I saw through your little game to give the Colonel his double contract. First you chuck away a trick with the King of Diamonds, and then you lead the Ten so that when the Colonel ducks, the suit is hopelessly blocked. But I put a stop to your scheme. I just overtook your Ten with my Knave and led a Heart, and even you hadn't the face not to make your Ace and Queen of Hearts and defeat the contract."

Sandy Hair laughed outright.

"And to think I was congratulating myself on having in you such a sound partner, while actually you overtook the Ten merely out of rage with me for throwing away tricks," he exclaimed. "Why, man, look at the hands. Don't you see that if I don't throw the King under the Ace, but merely try to unblock by throwing the Ten,

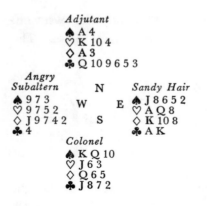

Adjutant
♠ A 4
♡ K 10 4
◇ A 3
♣ Q 10 9 6 5 3

Angry Subaltern
♠ 9 7 3
♡ 9 7 5 2
◇ J 9 7 4 2
♣ 4

Sandy Hair
♠ J 8 6 5 2
♡ A Q 8
◇ K 10 8
♣ A K

Colonel
♠ K Q 10
♡ J 6 3
◇ Q 6 5
♣ J 8 7 2

I dare not lead Diamonds when I get in with my high Clubs. For if I lead the King, it merely sets up the Colonel's Queen, and he makes his contract with four Club tricks, three Spades, and two Diamonds; while if I lead the Eight, he takes the trick with his Queen, and now the suit is completely blocked, and there's no way of giving you the lead. So I should have to play on Spades, but all the Colonel has to do is to lead dummy's small Diamond to set up his Queen."

"Yes, I'm beginning to understand," said the no-longer-angry Subaltern in a subdued but interested voice. "But what if the Colonel had not put up dummy's Ace on the first round?"

"In that case," replied the other, "I'd play my Ten. If the Colonel takes it with the Queen, as he almost certainly would, he would now be three tricks down. For on getting in with Clubs, I'd lead my Diamond King into dummy's lone Ace, and on getting the lead again with Clubs, I'd be able to put you in to make three Diamond tricks and then lead a Heart for me to make two tricks in that suit. If the Colonel refuses to take with the Queen, he still can't get his contract, as then he can't make more than one trick in the suit, and would have to play Hearts to me in the end."

48

"Yes," said the now completely humble Subaltern, "I know I have made a fool of myself. All I can do is to offer you my most abject apologies."

"Oh, that's all right. Don't give it another thought," returned Sandy Hair rather absently. "What I want you to realise is that, except in the variation where the declarer ducks the first trick in both hands, East must at all cost avoid taking a trick in Diamonds. It's really rather a remarkable hand, don't you think?"

And he looked round at the group of his fellow officers, who had been following his analysis intently. The Adjutant spoke:

"What we think is that this Mess has acquired itself a master bridge player and a very welcome comrade."

And the formerly angry Subaltern led the chorus of "Hear, hear's" and held out his hand to Sandy Hair.

* * *

"Well, that post mortem ended happily," remarked the Nine of Hearts in a gratified tone. Then he turned to me: "Why is it, Master Robert, that you humans so often hold disagreeable post mortems? You sit down to play a game as part of your social life. In many cases the players are friends, and in others club acquaintances who are at least supposed to be friendly. Yet how often you say cruel, hurtful, bitter things to each other when all you are discussing is the technique of a sport. In other sports, outdoor and indoor, nothing like that happens. Golfers, chess players, footballers and fishermen talk vehemently about their exploits—sometimes not too truthfully. But

49

they hardly ever allow their debates to become acrimonious, and seldom express themselves rudely or bitingly. Discussions of bidding and play can be of enthralling interest, and things of sheer intellectual delight can be discovered that way. Why, then, don't you humans just enjoy them, without so frequently making them accusatory, quarrelsome, and sometimes even the occasion for a broken friendship? Why is it, Master Robert?"

Quite at a loss to answer the kindly, puzzled little fellow, I shook my head mournfully in a manner I tried to make sapient, as who could say much if he wished. Before I had thought of some excuse to make for bridge humanity's frailty, the Four of Clubs interposed:

"It isn't a question of the money at stake," he said. "I have seen some of the worst displays of ill-temper and discourtesy at penny and threepenny games. And anyway palookas are generally much more offensive to each other than really good players. The less they know, the more they lay down the law to each other."

"That's quite true," replied the Nine of Hearts. "Ignorance always and everywhere tries to justify itself by emotional violence just because it is not really sure of itself. But with a good player, it should be different. Why should he not be content to make his point without turning it into a barb? Let me give you an example, Master Robert. The hand itself, too, is of no small interest. It was a case of the successful use of—"

AN UNLOADED PISTOL

(*The Tale of the Nine of Hearts*)

IT WAS AN ORDINARY CUT-IN GAME AT THE CLUB, AND
South and East were first-rate players, while West was
rather mediocre. South dealt:

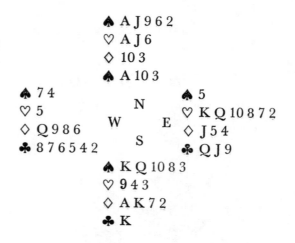

♠ A J 9 6 2
♡ A J 6
♢ 10 3
♣ A 10 3

♠ 7 4
♡ 5
♢ Q 9 8 6
♣ 8 7 6 5 4 2

N
W　E
S

♠ 5
♡ K Q 10 8 7 2
♢ J 5 4
♣ Q J 9

♠ K Q 10 8 3
♡ 9 4 3
♢ A K 7 2
♣ K

South opened with One Spade, and eventually Seven Spades was bid. West led the Eight of Clubs, and when dummy went down, South could see only twelve tricks. His singleton King took the first trick, dummy playing the Three and East the Nine. South drew a round of trumps with the King, and cashed the Ace and King of Diamonds. Then he ruffed a Diamond with dummy's Ace; returned to his hand with the Ten of trumps, East discarding the Ten of Hearts; and ruffed his last Diamond in dummy, East throwing the Heart Deuce.

The declarer now paused to count East's hand. East held originally three Diamonds and one Spade. The play to the first trick made it likely he held three Clubs— Queen-Knave-Nine. In which case he must have six Hearts, and his peter showed these were probably headed by the King-Queen. If this reading was correct, the position now was:

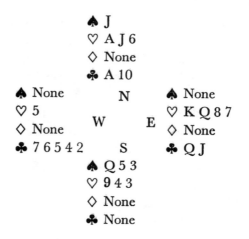

♠ J
♡ A J 6
◇ None
♣ A 10

♠ None   N   ♠ None
♡ 5   ♡ K Q 8 7
◇ None   W   E   ◇ None
♣ 7 6 5 4 2   S   ♣ Q J

♠ Q 5 3
♡ 9 4 3
◇ None
♣ None

With a sigh of regret that East's and West's hands were not interchanged, for then there would be a simple squeeze against West, South began to despair of finding a way to create the missing thirteenth trick. Suddenly a fantastic idea came to him. He pondered it a moment, and then set himself to carry it out. He cashed the Ace of Hearts, with a prayer that West's singleton would be a small card and tell no tales. Brigidda, the goddess of the game, gave him his wish, and West played the Five. The declarer led dummy's last trump, and overtook with the Queen, thus severing the last link with dummy and the Ace of Clubs. The declarer now played his last two trumps, and on the second of these East had to decide to discard from King of Hearts and Queen-Knave of Clubs. He reasoned thus:

"Declarer has probably one Heart and one Club left. It is clear my partner has no Club protection, since I alone have higher Clubs than dummy's Ten. On the other hand, my partner has a Heart left, if the declarer has a Heart and a Club, and it may well be the Nine. So I must keep my Club guard, and hope for my partner to have the best Heart."

So he discarded the King of Hearts, and I and my little brother, the Four of Hearts, made the twelfth and thirteenth tricks. It was a brilliant pseudo-squeeze by South, who presented at East's head a pistol East could not possibly know was not loaded.

But now I come to the point of my story. Did West, who knew East to be a much better player than he, realize what had happened? No. He merely saw what he thought was a chance to call East to book.

"What on earth made you discard all your Hearts," he demanded, angrily.

"I could not know you had only a singleton," replied East. "The cunning way South played made it seem certain he had a Club and a Heart left."

"If I had had two Hearts originally," retorted West, "I should have parted with my second Heart long ago."

And did East explain quietly and pleasantly why that would have been bad play? He did not. It was with contempt in his voice that he spoke:

"Excellent, indeed! If you had had two Hearts, then in the end-play the declarer would in fact have had the one Heart and one Club I credited him with. In which case your Heart discard would have transferred to me the task of protecting the Hearts as well as the Clubs. Then I should have been really squeezed. During the play I thought you didn't discard a Heart because you were playing well. Now your ingenuous confession means you were saved from going wrong only by lack of opportunity."

*   *   *

The Little Folk all looked at me to see how I was taking this attack on human nature.

"Well," I said, excusingly, "it was rather hard on East not only to be tricked legitimately by his opponent, but also upbraided wrongfully by his partner."

"Of course, it was," broke in the Ten of Diamonds. "The Heart tribe are too soft and sentimental for this tough world. They expect men to be angels. West asked for what he got. He should have known that a player as good as East evidently was would not have thrown away his King of Hearts without some good reason. Instead of flying into a rage, West should have courteously asked his partner for an explanation. Let me tell you of a case where a player who knew his partner was his superior at the game, did just that—even after his partner had been guilty of an outrageous breach of the Laws of Bridge and good manners."

DUMMY SPEAKS OUT OF TURN

(*The Tale of the Ten of Diamonds*)

YOU ALL KNOW DR. MCGUIRE—A FIERY OLD IRISHMAN, with a deep passion for the game, an uncontrollable temper whose outbursts are over in a moment, and a love for his fellow-men that few fail to reciprocate. Perennially smoking a long-stemmed pipe, his burly figure is seen in this club almost every day. He has won himself a privileged position, so that none objects when, as dummy, he sometimes strolls around to take a look at his partner's hand. In this club the Doc. can do no wrong. But the occasion I am going to tell you about was an exception.

His partner was a young architect named Woodman, who rather fancied his game, but had a great admiration for the old Irishman and his powers of analysis. Woodman dealt these hands:

The Doc

♠ Q 3
♡ 9 6 4
◊ **10** 3
♣ A 8 6 5 4 2

          N
    W   E
          S

♠ A K
♡ A J 10 7
◊ A J 9 6 2
♣ K 7

Woodman

The final contract was Three No-Trumps, with Woodman, sitting South, as declarer. West led the Five of Spades, and as soon as he had tabled his cards, Dr. McGuire walked round the table, took a glance at Woodman's hand, and at once returned to his seat, puffing excited clouds of smoke from his long pipe. The old boy, thought I, had evidently seen something worth seeing. But the others were too intent on their cards and too accustomed to the Doctor's rapid circumnavigation of the table, to take any notice.

On West's lead of the Five of Spades dummy played the Three, East the Eight, and Woodman took the trick with the King. There was a pause while young Woodman stared at the two hands and the old man stared at young Woodman with shining eyes. Then Woodman cashed the King of Clubs and crossed to dummy with the Ace of Clubs, both opponents following. At which procedure the old man emitted so dense a smoke-screen of approval that young Woodman had to wait a moment for it to clear. With the Doctor's eyes nearly popping out of his head, young Woodman leaned forward and stretched out his hand to pick me up and play me.

Then the unheard of happened. Dummy tapped the outstretched hand sharply with his pipe-stem, and shouted:

"Play a Club, ye young idiot. Play a Club!"

Woodman withdrew his hand as though the pipe-stem had been red-hot, and they all stared in shocked amazement at the old man. He was all remorse and apologies.

"It's disgraced entirely I am," he declared. "What in heaven came over me to act that way, I couldn't tell ye. Ye'll just have to forgive an old man for an uncontrollable temper that once so often makes him make a damned fool of himself. Wash out the hand, me boys, and deal again. That's all I can suggest."

Well, the Doc. was the Doc. So they forgave him, and had a redeal. But young Woodman, though his annoyance soon vanished, remained puzzled. The rubber ended, he and the Doc. cut out of the table. He took the old man aside, and said to him:

"Doc., I may be every kind of an idiot, as you said, but for the life of me I can't see why you wanted me to play a club. I know it would set up four Club tricks,

The Doc
♠ Q 3
♡ 9 6 4
◇ 10 3
♣ A 8 6 5 4 2

```
      N
  W       E
      S
```

♠ A K
♡ A J 10 7
◇ A J 9 6 2
♣ K 7
Woodman

but there's no entry in dummy to cash them."

"I'd rather you hadn't re-minded me of me shame, boy. You see I thought you were going to do the right thing, and I was disappointed when ye didn't. All you had to do to land the contract was to lead a third round of Clubs, and discard your Ace of Spades. True it is, you can never lead a Spade yourself to the Queen, but what the devil are your opponents to do now? If you can't lead a Spade, they *daren't*. So you have turned the seven Spades they hold from assets to liabilities. Whenever they get the lead, all they can play are the red suits, and that's just what you want. D'you see, me boy?"

And young Woodman saw—and thankfully.

* * *

"That is a pleasing story," said the King of Hearts benignly.

"Yes," took up the Ace of Hearts in his best electioneer-ing voice. "The Ten of Diamonds falls into error when he accuses us of the Heart tribe of expecting bridge players to act as angels. We People of the Pack, Master Robert, know how prone you humans are to annoyance, impatience and anger. We know the best of you have your sadistic impulses. How should we not know, seeing it is your thoughts and feelings which have engendered us? Super-

60

naturals though we are, we cannot fail to partake to some degree of both your failings and your virtues. So, too, do we know that these baser and anti-social emotions are generally controlled by you humans in other spheres of your life. That, you rightly pride yourselves, is part of the meaning of civilization. Why, then, should you give way to them only in the bridge room? Or if you find yourselves doing it once in a while, why not show contrition at once as that lovable old doctor did?"

"If somebody doesn't stop those Hearts," put in the Ten of Clubs, "they'll go on moralising for ever. There must be some outlet for the host of irritations that beset all humans, and I think the bridge room a very good place for that. For what goes on there is away from the main stream of life. A bridge club is a pleasant backwater whose activities do not affect the fate of nations or the course of the work-a-day world. And no bridge player really minds the accusations and recriminations. They don't touch his honour or his purse. They just let people blow off steam. Which is why in ordinary life bridge players are such harmless, easy-going folk."

"And I think it's high time we changed the subject," said the King of Spades in a lordly tone. "The point in the last story I found of most significance is that it did not occur to Woodman to discard the Ace of my tribe, although I had been played already, and my consort was in dummy, so that the Ace was of no special value to him. It is extraordinary how humans tend to cling to us high cards. Flattering, of course; but our real purpose is to be allowed to exert our power at the right moment. There is nothing more exasperating than to be treasured up by some well-meaning ass only in the end to be rendered impotent. It is an insult to one's kingship. I most emphatically do not agree with the Ace of Hearts and the rest of his tribe that folly at bridge is not deserving of anger just because it is a game and not some sordid trade."

Royal indignation shook the dignified little monarch, as he went on:

"I speak from suffering still new, for it was but yesterday that I was made the victim of—"

A MISSED OPPORTUNITY

(*The Tale of the King of Spades*)

IT WAS MY MISFORTUNE TO BE DEALT TO THAT TYPE OF player whose first thought is to protect his high cards from capture except when he follows the rule—all too easy for him to remember—of covering an honour with an honour. As his head cannot contain more than one idea at a time, if that, it never occurs to him that a person of my calibre does not ask to be cherished by fools, but prefers to be sacrificed in a daring effort to play a decisive part in the game—to make or mar a contract. And now watch what happened:

```
                    ♠ A 10 6
                    ♡ K 7 3 2
                    ◇ K 2
                    ♣ 10 8 7 4
  ♠ K 9 7 2            N          ♠ 8 5 3
  ♡ Q 10 8 4                      ♡ J 9
  ◇ 3          W          E       ◇ A J 10 9
  ♣ Q J 9 3          S            ♣ K 6 5 2
                    ♠ Q J 4
                    ♡ A 6 5
                    ◇ Q 8 7 6 5 4
                    ♣ A
```

South, who was a good player, found himself driven by his partner into the wishful contract of Five Diamonds, which East doubled. West led the Queen of Clubs, and as the declarer surveyed the 26 cards at his disposal, he could not but feel his task was rather hopeless. The loss of two or three trump tricks and one Heart trick seemed unavoidable, and it might well be that I, too, was lying in wait to take a trick in East's hand.

But to win at bridge you must never despair until you have to. South began to think. To lead trumps would be madness. The only possible chance was an end-play in trumps. So South set about shortening his hand. The Ace of Clubs took the first trick. South led the Four of Spades, and when West played low, finessed dummy's Ten. It held the trick, and I saw South's face brighten. Ruffing a small

64

Club in his hand, he led the Queen of Spades, and as West did not cover, my consort won that trick. The declarer now entered dummy with the Ace of Spades, and ruffed another Club. The King of Hearts was another entry to dummy for the declarer to ruff dummy's last Club. The Ace of Hearts was cashed, and declarer's last Heart led to the tenth trick.

At the end of the ninth trick East had played three Spades, two Hearts, and four Clubs. Only trumps were left him, so he was compelled to ruff the Heart. And whatever trump he now led, he could not make more than one other trick.

Thus the contract of Five Diamonds, doubled, was made, while, as you can all see, my numbskull missed the only opportunity he had of taking decisive action. At the second trick, when South led the Four of Spades, West should have boldly played me and so prevented the Ten of Spades from becoming an entry into dummy. South could have ruffed only two clubs, would have been unable to box East up at the end, and had no possible means of avoiding defeat. Only at trick two could West have evaded the passivity the declarer sought to impose on the defence, for, of course, at trick four it did not matter in the least whether West covered the lead of the Queen of Spades or not. West's idiotic refusal to protect his partner by sacrificing me, condemned me, the key-card of the whole hand, to fill the sterile roll of a mere spectator.

*　*　*

Polite murmurs of commiseration came from the gathering. It was plain that most of the Pack held the King of Spades in considerable awe. Then his Queen spoke;

65

"I think, my dear, you're a little hard on your numbskull. It was not so easy for him to tell as early as the second trick that by playing you he could kill the Ten in dummy as an entry. South might have held Queen-Knave-Five-Four in Spades. Then again suppose I or the Knave had been singleton in East's hand. Now if West played you and crashed the singleton honour in East's hand, West would actually set up the Ten as an entry."

"In the first case," snapped the King of Spades, "there is no play that could prevent the Ten being an entry; and in the second case South would have had five Spades, and the contract would more likely have been Four Spades than Five Diamonds. No, I can see no excuse for West. He knew from his hand that East had doubled mainly on trumps, and that therefore it would probably be vital to cut down the number of dummy's entry cards. His duty was to take any opportunity he could to drive out a high card in dummy."

At this point the Two of Spades stepped forward. He bowed low to his King and Queen.

"To wipe out the painful memory of the mishap that so undeservedly befell Your Majesty," he said in an eager, yet humble voice, "may I recall an incident in which Your Majesty shone by taking a trick in a highly unusual way?"

"You may," replied the King with a gracious smile. "But I would remind you it is nothing to us high personages to take a trick. We are accustomed to that. Almost I might say we are blasé where trick-taking is concerned. That is our job. As I have explained, what appeals to us is not trick-taking in itself, but to play a decisive role in the

66

destiny of a hand. Any one of us high cards would rather be sacrificed to that end than merely to be cashed in the ordinary course of events."

"In what I have to tell, Sire," answered the Two of Spades, "you both took a trick and made a sacrifice in that you condescended to do the work I, the lowliest of your subjects, generally do, and entrusted to me the honour of acting in your place. Which is why the event is my happiest memory and why I call it—"

AN EXCHANGE OF ROLES

(*The Tale of the Two of Spades*)

WE WERE FORTUNATE IN BEING DEALT TO A GOOD PLAYER,
thus:

```
              ♠ 10 9 7 6
              ♡ 6 2
              ◊ A J 10 8 3
              ♣ 5 4
♠ 5 4                              ♠ A J 8
♡ A J 9 8 7 3      N              ♡ K Q 10 5 4
◊ Q 7 2        W       E          ◊ K 5 4
♣ 8 6              S              ♣ 10 7
              ♠ K Q 3 2
              ♡ None
              ◊ 9 6
              ♣ A K Q J 9 3 2
```

An unusually interesting hand, and the bidding was
spirited and enterprising. South, who was vulnerable
against non-vulnerable opponents, was the dealer.

South	West	North	East
1 ♣	1 ♡	2 ◊	4 ♡
4 ♠	No bid	No bid	5 ♡
No bid	No bid	5 ♠	Double
No bid	No bid	No bid	

West led the Ace of Hearts, and South ruffed with the
Three of Spades, and led the Queen of trumps. East took
with the Ace, and returned a Heart. The declarer paused
for a moment, and looked at the two trumps left in his hand
—me and my Lord the King. My heart began to throb,
as I realised why he did not immediately send me forth on

my dull routine task of ruffing a card there was no fear would be over-ruffed.

Then came my great moment. The declarer chose you, Sire, to ruff the trick, leaving it to me to continue the unaccustomed task of drawing trumps. My Lord the King and I had exchanged roles, to his greater glory and to my infinite joy.

You perceive, of course, why the declarer had so acted. To protect the wonderful Club suit trumps must be drawn. Had the declarer ruffed with me, and then cashed my liege Lord, the Knave would not have fallen, and the declarer would have had to cross to dummy with the Ace of Diamonds to draw the last trump. On taking the trick with the Knave of trumps, whichever defender had it would defeat the contract by cashing a Diamond trick.

If the opposing trumps are split 4-1 contract cannot be made. So the declarer had only to consider a 3-2 division. Here two trump tricks must be lost, unless the Knave is doubleton. By unblocking the trump suit with the ruff with the King, the declarer gave up the chance of an overtrick, if the Knave had been doubleton, but ensured his contract. For when East had made his Knave of trumps, the declarer took the rest of the tricks with Clubs, the Ace of Diamonds, and dummy's long trump, on which South's losing Diamond was discarded.

Was not the tale worth telling, Sire, for both our sakes?

* * *

"Indeed it was," said the King, and he held out his hand to the gratified little Deuce, who bent over it and kissed it fervently. The King of Spades went on:

71

"It was also worth telling for the fine analysis by the declarer, who appreciated that there is no work too menial for us high personages if only that work be necessary to the right and proper direction of the play. No sacrifice then is too great."

There was a moment's respectful silence, and then the Seven of Diamonds spoke:

"We have been hearing a great deal about sacrifices, but so far it has always been just the sacrifice of a single card. I know of a case that puts all such paltry immolations in the shade. What think you, Master Robert, of the sacrifice of a whole suit? It happened about a year ago, and is without exception the most brilliant defence that has ever come my way. The circumstances, too, were rather diverting, for the defeat of the contract resulted in the humbling of—"

TWO SUPERCILIOUS KIBITZERS

(The Tale of the Seven of Diamonds)

NOT ALL OF YOU MAY KNOW PROFESSOR HARDACRE. HE HAS the Chair of Mathematics at the University near here, and comes only occasionally to this club for a game. His powers of analysis are at times as amazing as at other times is his ignorance of psychology. If a hand depends on sheer deduction, his play would make you think he had seen and minutely studied all four hands. He might be a great player were it not for his utter inability to disbelieve his opponents or ever

73

to take his partner's bidding with a grain of salt. To him the game is an exercise in probabilities and distribution, and he treats bidding and the fall of the cards as sources of pure scientific data. When bidding and play are honest, he shines; when they are deceptive, he can fall into the simplest of traps, and then appears as bewildered as a child. In the case I am going to relate his reasoning powers were fortunately able to have full scope.

There is one other thing to say before I get on with the story. Professor Hardacre is more than a bit deaf. But his infirmity varies. There are times when people have to raise their voices and speak very distinctly to him. At others—generally if there is no great background of noise—he seems scarcely deaf at all, which can be very disconcerting for those foolish enough to count on his not hearing low-spoken remarks.

On the occasion I tell of, it was early afternoon in the club, and there were only a couple of tables in play. Two of the younger members strolled in; glanced at the Professor's score-sheet; saw there was one game to the credit of the other side, and deciding they would soon be able to cut in at that table, sank into chairs just behind the Professor to look on till the rubber was over. They smiled slightly at each other, as if they rather thought to find their role of kibitzers entertaining.

They were of that bright, adventurous school which sets particular store on "making things hard for opponents" by bluff bidding and inordinate false-carding. The few times they had played at the Professor's table in the past they had seen him only as the disconcerted victim of their favourite

74

methods of creating uncertainty and confusion. So they exchanged glances of amused expectancy.

Professor Hardacre sat East, and South dealt these hands:

```
                    ♠ K Q 7 2
                    ♡ A Q 8 3
                    ◇ K
                    ♣ Q 5 3 2
        ♠ J 9 8 6              ♠ 5 4 3
        ♡ K J 10 9    N        ♡ 6 5
        ◇ 3        W     E     ◇ A Q J 8 7 6 2
        ♣ J 9 8 7     S        ♣ 10
                    ♠ A 10
                    ♡ 7 4 2
                    ◇ 10 9 5 4
                    ♣ A K 6 4
```

SOUTH	WEST	NORTH	EAST
1 ♣	No bid	1 ♡	3 ◇
No bid	No bid	3 ♠	No bid
3 N-T	No bid	No bid	4 ◇
No bid	No bid	4 N-T	No bid
No bid	No bid		

West led the Three of Diamonds; dummy's King went on; and the Professor fell into deep thought. The moments passed, and he made no move. The two young kibitzers grew impatient, and began to whisper.

"The dignity of a Chair in Higher Mathematics evidently demands the enhancement of slow-motion."

"I shouldn't have thought that either slow-motion or

75

```
              ♠ K Q 7 2
              ♥ A Q 8 3
              ♦ K
              ♣ Q 5 3 2
 ♠ J 9 8 6              ♠ 5 4 3
 ♥ K J 10 9      N      ♥ 6 5
 ♦ 3        W       E   ♦ A Q J 8 7 6 2
 ♣ J 9 8 7      S      ♣ 10
              ♠ A 10
              ♥ 7 4 2
              ♦ 10 9 5 4
              ♣ A K 6 4
```

logarithms were really essential to the taking of a King with an Ace."

"Or to the cashing of two more winners and trusting partner for the setting trick."

They smirked at each other's wit. But still Professor Hardacre pondered. They wondered at his indecision. Presently the whispering began again.

"Of course, it is true that to cash three Diamond tricks might squeeze partner, if he holds the other three suits, but does he?"

"If that's what the old boy fears, why not take with the Ace and lead something else—say a Spade or a Club?"

"That seems fair enough. But wait! I do believe he's going to play something and give us a chance of getting to the table."

The Professor stirred in his seat. Slowly his right hand rose, and from his Diamonds he firmly drew me and played me to the trick. I shall never forget the gasp of amazement that came from the two whisperers.

In silence they watched the play. Declarer took the trick, and made three Spade tricks, two Hearts, and three Clubs. But the tenth trick he could not make, as West held all the other three suits, and the declarer could develop nothing.

Professor Hardacre turned towards the two abashed young men, and lectured them in mild tones.

"Gentlemen," he said, "I trust you approve of my defence,

and that you forgive me for taking a little time to evolve it. You see, I had first to try to picture the distribution in terms of the bidding, which on this occasion appeared to me to be genuine." He directed a slightly satirical glance at the young men, and continued:

"South did not rebid his Clubs, nor did he support either his partner's Hearts or Spades. He passed on the second round. Over Three Spades he bid Three No-Trumps. Obviously my partner's lead was a singleton. From all this I deduced that South held four Diamonds to the Ten-Nine, four Clubs, and five cards in the two majors. Of course, he might have five Clubs and only four cards in the majors. In that case the contract could not be broken. But if North's distribution was echoed in West's hand, and he, too, had 4-4-4-1 division—as seemed likely although for two hands to hold this distribution in the same deal occurs only about once in a thousand deals—the contract might be defeated provided I did not squeeze him with my Diamonds and took steps to prevent South from squeezing him.

"Clearly I dared not take my three Diamond tricks. To do that would set up a Diamond trick for South and squeeze West's hand to impotence. But suppose West had just one trick in each of the other three suits. Dared I take my Ace of Diamonds as the setting trick, and then switch to Spades or Clubs? I concluded after some thought that I dared not. For all the declarer would have to do would be to play back a Diamond to me, presenting me with a trick, but squeezing West in the process. At that moment the declarer would have only eight sure tricks, but once the triple, progressive squeeze on West was started, the declarer would develop with ease the two extra tricks he needed. All we could make would be two Diamonds and a Heart or Three Diamonds.

"Let us follow one variation to the end, and I can assure you all the others work out similarly. I win the first trick with my Ace, and return a Spade. South wins with the Ace, and plays a Diamond—the Nine or Ten. I return another Spade, dummy's Queen takes, and declarer enters the closed hand with the Ace of Clubs; takes the Heart finesse in dummy; cashes the Ace of Hearts; and throws West in with a small Heart. West returns a Spade, dummy's King winning and South discarding a Diamond. Dummy's Eight of Hearts is played, South discarding his last Diamond, and West is squeezed in the black suits. At this stage the situation is:

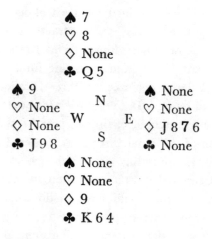

♠ 7
♡ 8
♢ None
♣ Q 5

♠ 9   N   ♠ None
♡ None   W   E   ♡ None
♢ None   S   ♢ J 8 7 6
♣ J 9 8   ♣ None

♠ None
♡ None
♢ 9
♣ K 6 4

"If on the lead of the Heart West throws his Spade, dummy's Eight makes, and the Queen and King of Clubs.

78

If he throws a Club, declarer makes three Club tricks."

"Therefore," concluded the Professor, "I decided I must not take even my Ace of Diamonds. By passing the first Diamond, I made it impossible for the declarer to play Diamonds in order to squeeze West. For if he does, I can then run my entire Diamond suit. I hope you find my analysis sound, gentlemen; and it did not, I assure you, involve the use of logarithmic tables."

The young kibitzers looked ashamed. Then they laughed, and one said: "Don't rub it in, Professor. We're beat."

* * *

Tiny cries of admiration greeted the end of the tale.

"Indeed a beautiful defence," said the Five of Hearts, "and inspired by a solicitude for partner's hand that few players could rise to. I suppose that is why the Professor took so long to decide. It's much simpler when one is protecting oneself against the threat of a squeeze."

"Not necessarily," retorted the Ten of Clubs. "I remember being dealt to a good player, who justifiably kept the table waiting quite as long as Professor Hardacre did, and his concern was his own hand. But I'll admit he had to guard against a double threat—a squeeze and a throw-in. He found the solution in the form of—"

A BRILLIANT LEAD

(*The Tale of the Ten of Clubs*)

TO BEGIN WITH I SHALL LET YOU SEE ONLY TWO HANDS—
my man's and dummy:

```
                ♠ 9 4
                ♡ K Q J 10 6
                ◇ 9 4 2
   My Man       ♣ 6 4 3
   ♠ Q J 7 5
   ♡ None          N
   ◇ K J 8 5 3   W   E
   ♣ A 10 9 2      S
```

NORTH	EAST	SOUTH	WEST
No bid	No bid	1 ♠	2 ◇
2 ♡	No bid	3 N-T	No bid
No bid	No bid		

My man, West, led the Deuce of Clubs. His partner
took the trick with the King, and returned the Knave of
the suit. South covered with the Queen, and West's Ace
made. He cashed the Nine of Clubs, all following; and
then he fingered me musingly. And as his eyes rested full
upon me, I could see his thoughts as plainly as if they were
goldfish swimming in a bowl. He was an unusually clear-
minded thinker.

"Just a moment, Club Ten," he was saying to himself.
"I'm not so sure I ought to cash you. Let's just have a look
around. What d'you suppose is South's hand? He must
surely have the Ace-King of Spades and the Aces of Hearts
and Diamonds, for without them he wouldn't have a hope
of making his contract. Distribution? Three Clubs, we
know, and almost certainly four Spades, for with five he
would have forced with Three Spades on the second round.
Then he has, I should think, either two Hearts and four

Diamonds or three of each. Anyway, he has eight tricks on top—five Hearts, two Spades, and a Diamond.

"Now what happens, if I cash you for the fourth trick, Club Ten? You wouldn't cause the enemy any trouble, as both hands can discard Diamonds. But what do I lead next? A Spade honour? South would take; cash his Diamond Ace; and play off dummy's Hearts. That would leave the Nine of Spades and Nine of Diamonds in dummy and, say, the Ace-Ten of Spades with South. I should be squeezed in Spades and Diamonds, unless East has the guarded Queen of Diamonds. But if South should have four Diamonds—which seems most likely—East can have only one, and the squeeze would work. Yes, that's the danger. Now what can I do about it?"

The other players and one or two lookers-on began to stir restively. Unperturbed, my man's thoughts proceeded on their logical way.

"If South has the Ace-Queen of Diamonds, the contract is cold, unless East has the Ten of Spades. But I don't think South has the Ace-Queen of Diamonds. If he had, he would more likely have opened with One No-Trumps on his balanced hand than One Spade. My best chance is to assume South's hand is four Spades to the Ace-King-Ten and four Diamonds to the Ace, and that East has the Queen of Diamonds. In that case, I'm not going to play you, tempting as you are, my dear Club Ten. At the moment South has two losing tricks. I'm not going to rectify the count for him to squeeze me. Let him do his own dirty work—if he can."

By now every eye was fixed wonderingly on my man. Suddenly he realised it.

"Sorry for the trance," he said, "but this wants a little thought."

There were reluctant grunts of acquiescence. He returned to his pondering.

"Well, then, what shall I lead? A Spade honour? South would simply throw me in at the eleventh trick with a Diamond, and make me play Spades up to his Ace-Ten. I can't lead a small Spade, for that would give him his extra trick at once. Well, that means I must lead a Diamond. A small one? Not on your life! Partner would play his hypothetical Queen, and the declarer would seize the opportunity to reduce his two losing tricks to one by ducking and leaving East in the lead. Then South could squeeze me in Diamonds and Spades as before. Yes, my course is clear."

At this point he led the King of Diamonds, exclaiming mentally:

"Now let South duck if he likes, and then I'll make the setting trick with you, my faithful Ten of Clubs!"

The complete deal was:

```
                  ♠ 9 4
                  ♡ K Q J 10 6
                  ◇ 9 4 2
                  ♣ 6 4 3
  ♠ Q J 7 5           N        ♠ 8 6 2
  ♡ None                       ♡ 8 7 5 4 3 2
  ◇ K J 8 5 3   W       E      ◇ Q
  ♣ A 10 9 2          S        ♣ K J 5
                  ♠ A K 10 3
                  ♡ A 9
                  ◇ A 10 7 6
                  ♣ Q 8 7
```

And my man had found in the strange lead of the King from King-Knave the only play that could defeat the contract.

*　　*　　*

"That's all very well," said the Six of Clubs, as his brother Ten ceased speaking. "But suppose after all South had held four Diamonds to the Ace-Queen and East the Ten of Spades. It's by no means improbable on the bidding. In that case the lead of the King of Diamonds gives away the contract, which the lead of a Spade would defeat."

"I know, I know," replied the Club Ten impatiently; "but my man had to take a view. He had often played with South before, and knew his ways. He felt pretty confident that if South had held the Diamond tenace and only two small Spades to the Ace-King, he would have opened with One No-Trumps and not with One Spade."

"Don't try to spoil a good story, Six," said the Ace of Clubs, in a peremptory voice. "It was a brilliant lead, and would still have been so even if it had failed."

The Club Six subsided. The short silence that followed the rebuke was broken by the Queen of Spades.

"We've just been given two examples of excessively slow play," she said, "and both the protagonists were men. I think you'll hardly ever find a really long trance at the bridge table by a woman. I wonder why."

"Women don't take the game so seriously," volunteered the Seven of Diamonds. "Women are realists, and can't forget that bridge is a game. So they never quite lose themselves in the intricacies of a situation. At the back of their minds is always the thought: 'What does it matter?' But for men, whatever they are doing at the moment overshadows everything else. Unlike women, they have no scale of values. Whatever they do is of first importance. So no effort seems misplaced, no inconvenience too great to impose on others, if only the outcome be success. A woman's social sense wouldn't let her keep the table waiting to irritation for her decision."

"I don't agree," said the Eight of Spades. "My gracious Queen is right—women don't go into long trances of thought at the bridge table. But the reason is that they don't have to. A woman's sense of intuition is far more highly developed than a man's. That is common knowledge. In ordinary life she acts partly by intuition and partly by reason. She is no different at the bridge table. Generally, she acts intuitively first, and then begins to reason when the initial intuitive impulse has exhausted itself."

"I was not aware you were an expert in psychology—and feminine psychology at that," put in the Knave of Spades, with a hint of jealousy in his tone. "But what is all this leading up to?"

"A concrete case to prove—or at least illustrate—what I have been saying," replied the Spade Eight. "I shall call it—"

AN INTUITIVE FINESSE
(*The Tale of the Eight of Spades*)

IN A DRAWING-ROOM WERE ONE MAN AND SEVEN WOMEN playing bridge. The man's wife had rung him up at his office just after luncheon, and told him her bridge party was threatened with disaster. One of her guests had failed her at the last moment.

"There'll be only one table instead of two," she moaned; "and even if I don't play at all, there'll be two women sitting out all the time. If things aren't too busy with you, do be a dear and save my party by taking the afternoon off and making up my two tables."

So here he was—the only man at a women's bridge afternoon. What was it going to be like? He had an idea that when women played bridge among themselves, there was little play and much talk about clothes and gossip about people. Disillusionment soon came.

He glanced at the partner he had cut, and saw a neatly dressed young woman still in her twenties, who was attractive in a sophisticated way and very efficient-looking. His opponents were rather older and less attractive, but it was evident that what was uppermost in the minds of all three was—bridge.

His partner, South, dealt and bid One Club.

```
                    ♠ K J 2
                    ♡ K J 5 3
                    ◇ K Q J 10
                    ♣ 10 9
    ♠ 10 9 7 6              ♠ Q 5 4
    ♡ Q 10 9 8 7    N       ♡ 4
    ◇ A 9 4      W     E    ◇ 7 6 5 2
    ♣ 3             S       ♣ Q 7 6 5 4
                    ♠ A 8 3
                    ♡ A 6 2
                    ◇ 8 3
                    ♣ A K J 8 2
```

West instantly bid One Heart. The man paused a few moments, and then went straight to Three No-Trumps. East passed, and South quite casually bid the Small Slam in Clubs. East doubled, and South promptly redoubled.

West led the Ten of Spades, and the man tabled his hand, feeling rather bewildered at the rapidity of the auction.

Play proceeded at the same breathless pace. Dummy's Knave was put on; East covered with the Queen; South's Ace took the trick. She led a Diamond, and when West ducked, continued with another Diamond. This trick West took, and, fearing lest South might have a losing Heart which she could discard on Diamonds, led the Ten of Hearts. My young woman smartly finessed dummy's Knave; led the Ten of trumps, and ran it when East played low. The Nine of Clubs was then led and run, and when West threw a Heart, South remarked equably.

"H'm, so the trump position is as bad as that, is it?"

Then for the first time she paused, and considered what next to do. She did not hesitate for long. After a few minutes I saw a slight smile curve her lips. With a quick movement of decision, she cashed dummy's two high Diamonds, throwing on them her Ace of Hearts and her last small Heart. The position now was:—

```
                    ♠ K 2
                    ♡ K 5 3
                    ◊ None
                    ♣ None
        ♠ 9 7                      ♠ 5 4
        ♡ Q 9 8       N            ♡ None
        ◊ None    W       E        ◊ None
        ♣ None        S            ♣ Q 7 6
                    ♠ 8 3
                    ♡ None
                    ◊ None
                    ♣ A K J
```

Dummy's King of Hearts was led, and now it was East's turn to hesitate. She saw, to her horror, that if she discarded a Spade, dummy's King of Spades would next be cashed, and then she would be left with her three trumps under South's three winning trumps, while the lead would still be in dummy. So East ruffed the Heart King with a small trump. South led the King of trumps, West and dummy throwing Hearts.

Now South led the Ace of trumps, and West was in trouble. As East was void of Hearts, West dared not part with her last Heart. So she discarded a Spade, and dummy's last Heart went on the trick. My young woman led the Three of Spades; West's Nine fell; dummy's King made; and I became the highest Spade, and took the last trick. All my young woman had lost was the Ace of Diamonds.

She leaned back in her chair with a quiet look of triumph in her eyes. The man gazed at her in amazement.

"Marvellously played!" he said. "But tell me one thing. At the moment that you took the Heart finesse, it seemed wholly unnecessary to worry to do so. Yet you reached quite decidedly for the Knave, though you were playing much too quickly at the time to have considered the matter. Did you realise then that the contract can't be made without that finesse?"

She laughed lightly.

"No," she said, "I didn't. Not just then. I sort of felt it might be a good idea to have as many entries as possible in dummy. But it was lucky I did, wasn't it? For I was able to threaten East with a trump coup by throwing away my

Hearts; and when she evaded that, I was able to squeeze West, as after the first trick the protection of the Spade suit had passed from East to West. I wasn't sure of that, of course, but I had to try it."

* * *

"An entertaining narrative," pronounced the Knave of Spades. He added, with a touch of sarcasm: "But it is a pity West's intuition didn't suggest to her the lead of a Heart, despite East's double, for then nothing can save South from losing the Ace of Diamonds and a Heart ruff."

The Eight of Spades started to reply rather hotly, when his brother, the Six, was noticed to be laughing aloud to himself in a curiously delighted way. All the Little People stared at him. He sobered down at once.

"Sorry," he said, "but all this talk of reason and intuition reminds me of what happened to Professor Hardacre's friend who once came to this club for a game. It was really rather amusing.

"Tell us about it," I said.

"Very well, Master Robert," he replied. "You know how club secretaries are always the soul of tact and equal to every occasion. Well, this was the only time I've ever seen—"

A CLUB SECRETARY DISCONCERTED
(*The Tale of the Six of Spades*)

DINNER WAS NEARLY OVER, AND THE CLUB SECRETARY HAD wandered into the card-room to see that everything was in readiness for the evening session, when one of the stewards came in to say there was a visitor at the front door asking for the Secretary.

"All right, show him in here," said that official.

A tall man entered the room. I judged him to be in the early thirties, but he was one of those people who are born old, and whose age is almost impossible to guess within ten or fifteen years. A solemn-faced, dry, humourless individual, but with an engaging simplicity of manner. Like his friend, Professor Hardacre, he was wise in some things and childlike in others.

He explained that he was a Lecturer in Logic and Statistics at the University, and that the Professor had recommended the club to him. Might he have a game?

"Certainly," said the Club Secretary. "We'll be starting up very shortly, and you may join in with pleasure. Have you played bridge much? Where do you generally play?"

"I have never played in my life," said the stranger. "But Professor Hardacre is very fond of the game, and I thought I would like to see if I, too, could obtain pleasure from it. So he lent me a book—one of the best, he said. I've studied it carefully, and now I want to play a rubber or two to discover whether or not it is an enjoyable pastime."

The Club Secretary was taken aback.

"I'm afraid in that case," he said, " I daren't let you play here. I'm awfully sorry, but, you see, the standard of play in this club is rather high. It's not at all the place for a beginner. I suggest you get Professor Hardacre to arrange a private game for you for practice."

"But," said the Lecturer in Logic, in a surprised voice, "I've read all about it, and it seems quite a simple game. Let me play just one rubber to see what it is like. You can be a spectator, and if you think I am unfit to play here, stop the game at once."

At first the Club Secretary was obdurate, but the stranger looked so disappointed that when three members presently strolled in, the Secretary explained matters to them, and they good-naturedly agreed to play a rubber with the Lecturer in Logic.

He dealt the first hand as East, with the Club Secretary sitting watchfully at his side.

$$\spadesuit \text{ A Q 9}$$
$$\heartsuit \text{ K 9 5 2}$$
$$\clubsuit \text{ Q 8}$$
$$\diamondsuit \text{ K 8 6 2}$$ *The Stranger*

♠ J 5 4 2		N	♠ K 10 6
♡ 8 6	W	E	♡ 10 4
◇ 10 5 4 3		S	◇ A Q J 9
♣ 7 6 5			♣ A K 4 2

$$\spadesuit \text{ 8 7 3}$$
$$\heartsuit \text{ A Q J 7 3}$$
$$\diamondsuit \text{ 7}$$
$$\clubsuit \text{ J 10 9 3}$$

EAST	SOUTH	WEST	NORTH
1 ◇	1 ♡	No bid	1 N-T
2 ♣	2 N-T	No bid	3 ♡
No bid	4 ♡	No bid	No bid
No bid			

West led the Three of Diamonds. Dummy's King was played, and the stranger took the trick with his Ace. He looked hard at dummy; glanced again at his own hand; then he threw his head back, and stared at the ceiling. The other three players observed him with amused tolerance, while the Club Secretary's face grew red with embarrassment as the stranger continued to consult the ceiling. Then, to my astonishment, he suddenly brought his eyes down to

```
              ♠ A Q 9
              ♡ K 9 5 2
              ♢ K 8 6 2
              ♣ Q 8           The Stranger
  ♠ J 5 4 2                  ♠ K 10 6
  ♡ 8 6          N           ♡ 10 4
  ♢ 10 5 4 3   W   E         ♢ A Q J 9
  ♣ 7 6 5        S           ♣ A K 4 2
              ♠ 8 7 3
              ♡ A Q J 7 3
              ♢ 7
              ♣ J 10 9 3
```

his own cards, seized hold of me, and awkwardly placed me on the table.

At once the Club Secretary rose.

"I'm really very sorry," he said firmly, "but I must stop the game, as you agreed I should. I can't allow this to go on, and these gentlemen's time to be wasted."

"Have I done something wrong?" stammered the Lecturer in Logic.

"You have only led from your favourably placed King right into a major tenace," said the Club Secretary.

The stranger gasped out:

"But that is the only lead that—"

"I'm sorry," the Club Secretary interrupted him. "But I warned you what might happen. You must accept my decision."

"Oh, I do," the stranger hastened to say, as he rose to his feet. "But I wish I knew where I was wrong. I thought —"

"Never mind about that," said the Club Secretary, soothingly. He was anxious to avoid a scene. "You come along to my office and have a chat."

"Thank you. Certainly," the other replied, absently as he picked up dummy's cards and the turned trick. "But first may I have your cards, gentlemen."

Wonderingly, they gave him over their hands. Thanking them and bowing courteously, he followed the Secretary into his office. There the official continued his apologies and soothing words. But the Lecturer in Logic was not listening. He was setting the four hands out on the Secretary's desk. Presently he turned, and said quietly:

"I was right. Look. My lead was the only one that defeats the contract."

The Club Secretary smiled.

"Let me explain," continued the Lecturer in Logic. "I read my partner's lead as fourth-high. In that case South's Seven must be a singleton. On his bid of Hearts I placed him with five to the Ace, so there was no trump trick for us. His bid of Two No-Trumps marked him with a Club stopper—probably four to the Knave-Ten. If that was so, he could, with the help of dummy's Queen, set up two Club tricks on which to discard two of dummy's Spades. In that way he would make his contract, losing only two Clubs and the Ace of Diamonds.

"The only hope, it seemed to me, was for the defence to make a Spade trick. But for that to happen Spades must be attacked at once. To let South first ruff a Diamond, would result in his taking out trumps and leading a Club, and it would then be one tempo too late for East to attack Spades. The Six was the right Spade to lead because it was vital to discover if West held the Knave. If he did not, East, on regaining the lead with a Club, must then try Diamonds in the faint hope of another trick in that suit. Don't you now think I was right?"

He looked appealingly at the Club Secretary. That conscientious official was red once more to the ears. He held out his hand.

"I apologise," he said. "Come back with me into the card-room and let me put matters right with the others. You're the most amazing beginner there has ever been, and this Club is going to be proud of you."

The Lecturer in Logic and Statistics took the outstretched hand, but shook it in farewell.

"No," he said, with a faint smile. "I thank you for your courtesy and generosity, but somehow I don't think I'd find bridge enjoyable. I'm afraid it's rather too obvious and easy a game to appeal to me. Anyway, I never did like games. But if I change my mind, I will certainly return one day to your very pleasant club."

* * *

He bowed solemnly to the disconcerted Club Secretary and went from the club. I've never seen him since.

Most of my little friends were with the Spade Six in looking upon his story as highly amusing, but a few did not join in the laughter. The minority view was roundly given expression by the King of Diamonds.

"The impudence of the fellow!" he fumed, with regal disdain, "So his Logical Lordship inferred simplicity for the infinite variety of the game, and his Statistical Eminence assumed his own superiority over the myriads of players he had never met—all on the strength of one single deal! He would have been bored, forsooth! if he had taken up this childish pastime! In the words of a great monarch who ruled in the world of mortals, 'We are not amused.'"

"I agree," declared the Queen of Hearts. "I think it was a pity the first hand he had to tackle was not a contract that could be made only by means of a Vienna Coup or some other play or something really complicated like that. He might have sung a different tune. But then, I suppose, the Six of Spades would have had no tale to tell. I wonder if Mr. Brilliant Beginner would have deduced the proper defence in a deal I am reminded of by the hand he played. There was just one right card to lead to reduce the declarer to helplessness by—"

DISRUPTING COMMUNICATIONS

(*The Tale of the Queen of Hearts*)

THE MAN I WAS DEALT TO WAS A VERY NICE PERSON. I FELT
he was nice the moment his fingers touched me as he arranged his hand. But, by the same token, I knew him to be
no master at the game. He had some knowledge and skill,
but was one of those who suffer from the things the Knave
of Spades is always talking about—phobias, complexes, inhibitions. He was always afraid of something. He suspected
his partners and opponents alike of false-carding, and his

particular dread was that he might anger his partner by failing to appreciate and fall in with his line of defence.

But he was a very nice person, and that is my excuse for what I did. This was the deal, with my young man and me at East:

```
                    ♠ 7
                    ♡ A K J 9
                    ◇ K Q 8 4
                    ♣ K 10 6 4
     ♠ J 9 8 5 3          N          ♠ Q 10 6 2
     ♡ 7 4                            ♡ Q 6 5 3 2
     ◇ 7 6 3        W         E       ◇ A 10 2
     ♣ Q 5 2              S           ♣ A
                    ♠ A K 4
                    ♡ 10 8
                    ◇ J 9 5
                    ♣ J 9 8 7 3
```

NORTH	EAST	SOUTH	WEST
1 ◇	Double	Redouble	1 ♠
2 ♡	2 ♠	3 ♣	No bid
4 ♣	No bid	5 ♣	No bid
No bid	No bid		

Don't ask me why North opened with One Diamond instead of One Heart. I can only suppose he was one of those pernicious people who reverse merely to show strength, instead of distribution plus strength. However, I was not interested in the bidding.

West led the Seven of Hearts, and dummy's Ace took the trick, South playing the Eight. The declarer entered his

102

hand with the King of Spades, and led the Knave of Clubs. West played low and so did the table, my young man's singleton Ace making.

And now he began to ruminate, fingering his cards nervously. How ought he to play? He felt this was the crucial moment for the defence. Was West's lead a singleton and South's Eight a false card? Or perhaps it was South's Eight that had been lone, and West had, with some crafty intent, led his middle card from Ten-Seven-Four. His fearfulness made him think this might well be so. In which case a Heart return would be fatal. But perhaps it was more likely that West's lead was singleton, and West would be very angry if he (East) failed to give him a Heart ruff. At the same time a Diamond lead looked inviting. If West should have the Knave, that would be fine, for then he (East) would be left with the Diamond tenace over dummy's remaining high honour.

As he went on in this kind of way, while the table waited patiently, I grew irritated at his doubts and fears, but was filled with compassion for his helplessness. He really was a very nice person. So I fell to the temptation—I acted for him. I waited till his restless fingering came near me, and then I gave a little jump and fell to the table face upward. The young man gazed at me in astonishment. But he was relieved at having the decision taken from him, and said nothing.

The declarer had no choice but to take the trick in dummy, and now there was no good lead from the table. I had well and truly prepared the way for an overruff of Hearts by West, and the declarer could not get back into his own

```
              ♠ 7
              ♡ A K J 9
              ◇ K Q 8 4
              ♣ K 10 6 4
♠ J 9 8 5 3        N        ♠ Q 10 6 2
♡ 7 4                       ♡ Q 6 5 3 2
◇ 7 6 3     W       E       ◇ A 10 2
♣ Q 5 2            S        ♣ A
              ♠ A K 4
              ♡ 10 8
              ◇ J 9 5
              ♣ J 9 8 7 3
```

hand to prevent it. Had I allowed my nice young man to return a small Heart, South's Ten would have held the trick. West would have been finessed through in trumps, and the contract made.

South did try to get back into his hand by playing a small Diamond from the table towards his Knave, but my timorous protege was by now awake to what I had done for him, and he went up at once with the Ace, and led another Heart. South ruffed; West overruffed with the Queen; and the contract was broken, the defence making the overruff and the Aces of Clubs and Diamonds.

You notice that the defence was somewhat similar to that made by the Lecturer man, but more subtle. Both were returns up to a tenace in dummy, but here a small card would have been fatal. Only by me could the link between dummy and the closed hand be broken.

*　　*　　*

An uneasy silence fell on the Little People, and I caught exchanges of meaning looks. Then the Ace of Hearts—pontificating as all the Aces seemed to do—addressed his Queen.

"Your tale, Mam, confesses to a lapse which, as Your Majesty is well aware, should have been reported to me. I do not recollect that you—"

"Oh, but it was—I did," the Queen hastened to assure him. "It happened a year or two ago, and I suppose your Excellency has forgotten. I just reported the bare fact of what I did. I didn't worry your Excellency with the whole story. But it was all properly entered up at the time —really it was."

"I crave your pardon, Mam," replied the Ace. "I did not realise that the *fait accompli* with which you faced us was also *chose jugee.*"

"That's all right," said the Queen, comfortably, as she held out a forgiving hand for him to bend over and kiss.

Seeing all was now well, the Wee Folk were once more chattering amiably to each other in undertones. The Ace of Hearts answered the puzzled look of inquiry I directed towards him.

That was an administration matter of domestic politics, Master Robert," he said apologetically. "I regret I had to obtrude it before you, but for us it was of prime importance."

"I'm sure it was," I said. "But I am interested. Would your Excellency be so good-natured as to enlighten me?"

"It's this way, Master Robert," he replied. "We do not absolutely forbid the use of our magic powers for or against you humans in the course of play, for that would be to deny our own natures. To be endowed with the gift of magic and never use it would not make sense. But we have to ensure that the exercise of our powers is strictly controlled within prescribed limits. You see, *our* existence depends on the continued existence of the game; and that would certainly be imperilled if the normal course of bidding and play were too often interfered with. Once in a while there is no harm done by a card dropping face upward on the table; and if it turns out to be just the right card to enable 'a very nice person' to make or break a contract—well, that is just a coincidence. But you couldn't have cards falling all over the table like leaves in an autumn wind, some of them helping 'very nice persons' and others proving the undoing of persons not so nice who happen to have earned the enmity of this or that inhabitant of the Pack, now could you?

"So we have a Law, enforced by severe penalties, that every time any one of us does give way to temptation, he or she must report it within twenty-four hours to the Ace of his or her tribe. Statistics of our interventions are thus carefully compiled. If we find any particular citizen of the Pack is indulging in his caprice too often, he is ordered to amend his behaviour. If the general average of interventions shows signs of dangerous increase, the four Kings at once issue jointly a Royal Proclamation, sometimes merely warning the Pack to exercise restraint, sometimes putting into effect one of our several systems of rationing, and occasionally totally prohibiting interventions for a period. So you see, Master Robert, why I was so disturbed when I thought no less a personage than the Queen of our tribe had omitted to report her little act of gracious kindness."

I replied that I saw that—and a great many other things as well that had been mysteries to me before.

"Yes," put in the Five of Diamonds, "we've helped you on occasions, Master Robert. Haven't you at times found yourself staring at your hand, quite undecided what to play in some really critical situation, and suddenly felt your eyes drawn irresistibly to one of us? It seemed, didn't it, as though the decision had been taken from you? You played the card, didn't you, and with success? That was our magic. But I'll say this for you, Master Robert—you don't often need it."

I bowed my acknowledgment of the compliment. The Diamond Five went on:

"Unfortunately, even our magic won't work when the key card is in dummy. One can't drop accidentally out of dummy, and lack of contact with your fingers makes it impossible to direct attention to the right card. Do you remember that slam hand I tried to keep you from going wrong over? It was not so long ago. I was in dummy, worse luck! Do you remember?

Astonished, I said I could not recall such a hand.

"Let me remind you of it," he persisted. "You played in masterly style up to a point, and then you came to grief. It was—"

A CASE OF IMPATIENCE

(*The Tale of the Five of Diamonds*)

YOU WERE SITTING SOUTH, MASTER ROBERT, AND YOU HAD
bid to Six Clubs.

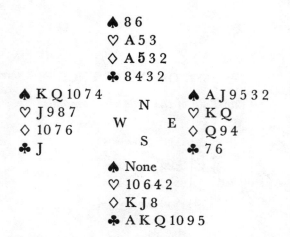

♠ 8 6
♡ A 5 3
◇ A 5 3 2
♣ 8 4 3 2

♠ K Q 10 7 4   ♠ A J 9 5 3 2
♡ J 9 8 7   N   ♡ K Q
◇ 10 7 6 W   E ◇ Q 9 4
♣ J   S   ♣ 7 6

♠ None
♡ 10 6 4 2
◇ K J 8
♣ A K Q 10 9 5

Both your opponents had called Spades, and West started with the King of that suit. You, Master Robert, ruffed
cleverly with the Nine of Clubs, so as to keep a trump entry
on the table. Now you cashed the Ace of trumps, dropping
West's Knave. Then you crossed to dummy with the Ace of
Hearts, East giving the Queen. You led dummy's Deuce of
Diamonds, and finessed your Knave. It worked. You re-
entered dummy by leading your Five of trumps to the
Eight, West throwing a Spade. You now ruffed dummy's
last Spade, and cashed first the King and then the Ace of
Diamonds. All followed in Diamonds, so I became the
master thirteenth.

Both technically and psychologically your play so far had
been excellent. From the very first trick you planned a
throw-in. You planned to strip your hand and dummy of
Diamonds and Spades and then concede a trick to an opponent's high Heart on the second round of the suit. If he
should happen to have no other Heart, you would make

your contract, as he would then have only Spades to lead from, and you could ruff in your own hand while discarding dummy's last Heart. You played the Heart Ace early and before ruffing dummy's last Spade. That was fine psychology indeed. At that stage it was unlikely that either opponent with a doubleton high Heart would foresee he might be end-played with it. You were lucky, too, in finding the guarded Diamond Queen in the East hand.

So far, so good then. At this point, after eight tricks, dummy had two trumps, two small Hearts, and me. In your own hand you held two trumps and three Hearts. The lead was in dummy with the Ace of Diamonds. And what happened? Your downfall. You were too impatient, Master Robert—impatient to cash me, the thirteenth Diamond. I tried to will you not to play me, but, being in dummy, there was nothing I could do about it. You picked me up and played me; and East, who now at this late stage had no difficulty in perceiving the danger of his position, threw his King of Hearts on me, and your contract was lost. You could no longer prevent West from making two tricks with his Knave-Nine of Hearts.

The pity of it! The moment had been ripe for your carefully schemed throw-in. All you had to do, Master Robert, instead of playing me, was to lead one of dummy's Hearts to East's King, and East, willy-nilly, would have given you that precious ruff-and-discard.

*   *   *

As the Diamond Five ended his tale. I became aware that black looks were being directed at him from all sides. Most

111

of the kindly small creatures thought it was no way to treat an honoured guest by reminding him of one of his failures. I realised I must be tactful in my comments if I was to keep the jolly little Five of Diamonds out of trouble. Clearly, he had meant no harm. Friendliness and bonhomie beamed from his tiny elfin face.

So I smiled genially and, I hope, without any trace of embarassment, and remarked that it was a habit of mine once in a while to do just that thing—play a hand quite well up to a point, and then relax my attention prematurely and spoil it all by some foolish slip. I added that I still could not recall that particular hand, which showed there was some truth in the cynical definition of memory as "that faculty by means of which a bridge player is able to reconstruct to the last card his past successes."

Whereat there was general laughter, and the awkward moment passed. But it was evidently thought that the sooner the subject of conversation was changed, the better, and I noticed a group of smaller Clubs push forward one of their number—the Five. The gnomish little fellow at once began to speak volubly. It seemed the idea was that the harm they imagined one Five had done, another Five was to undo. He addressed me directly:

"The Queen of Hearts said she would have liked the Lecturer in Logic to have met with a complicated Vienna Coup in the one and only hand he ever played. I was recently involved in one of the prettiest Vienna Coups you've ever seen, Master Robert. You'll like it, for it is just the sort of thing you yourself revel in executing."

I saw through the ingenuous flattery, but to please the ugly little sprite I pretended to swallow it with relish. He went on eagerly:

"The play is as complicated as the Queen of Hearts could wish. The whole thing had to be foreseen and planned for from the start, and it involved—"

AN EARLY THROW-IN AND VIENNA COUP
(*The Tale of The Five of Clubs*)

THE CALLING PLACED THE ADVERSE HIGH CARDS FOR THE
declarer, but the way in which he availed himself of that
knowledge and the use he made of me to put his scheme into effect have fixed the hand forever in my memory. It is

not often that we small cards are given real and decisive work to do. East dealt these cards:

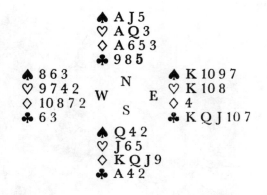

♠ A J 5
♡ A Q 3
◇ A 6 5 3
♣ 9 8 5

♠ 8 6 3
♡ 9 7 4 2
◇ 10 8 7 2
♣ 6 3

♠ K 10 9 7
♡ K 10 8
◇ 4
♣ K Q J 10 7

♠ Q 4 2
♡ J 6 5
◇ K Q J 9
♣ A 4 2

EAST	SOUTH	WEST	NORTH
No bid	No bid	No bid	1 ◇
Double	Redouble	No bid	No bid
2 ♣	2 N-T	No bid	3 N-T
Double	No bid	No bid	No bid

West led the Six of Clubs; dummy's Eight covered; South's Ace took East's Ten. The declarer crossed to the table with the Ace of Diamonds, and led—what do you think? Me. Yes at the third trick he began the end-play by using me to throw East in the lead. Is that to your liking, Master Robert?

Well, East looked pleased, and gleefully ran off his four Clubs, dummy discarding two Diamonds, and South the Deuce of Spades and the Five of Hearts. With his two remaining Kings lying snugly behind dummy's two remaining

116

Aces, it all looked safe enough to East. After the Clubs had
been cashed the situation was:

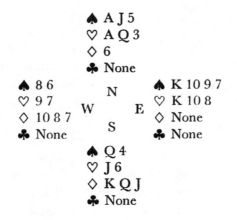

♠ A J 5
♡ A Q 3
◊ 6
♣ None

♠ 8 6
♡ 9 7
◊ 10 8 7
♣ None

♠ K 10 9 7
♡ K 10 8
◊ None
♣ None

♠ Q 4
♡ J 6
◊ K Q J
♣ None

East led the Seven of Spades, hoping to find the Queen
with West. But South had the Queen, and took the trick
with it. He then led the Six of Hearts, and put up dummy's
Ace, thus making East's King the Master card of the suit—
the Vienna Coup. The declarer returned to the closed hand
with dummy's last Diamond, and cashed the last two high
Diamonds, discarding the Queen and Three of Hearts from
the Table. What could East do? He had either to throw the
master King of Hearts or unguard his King of Spades. Hoping that West might have the Knave of Hearts, East threw
the King of that suit. The declarer then made the last two
tricks with the Knave of Hearts and dummy's Ace of
Spades.

Was that not an elegant Vienna Coup? But the whole
play has charm. The declarer had seven certain winners—

```
              ♠ A J 5
              ♥ A Q 3
              ♦ A 6 5 3
              ♣ 9 8 5
  ♠ 8 6 3              ♠ K 10 9 7
  ♥ 9 7 4 2    N       ♥ K 10 8
  ♦ 10 8 7 2  W   E    ♦ 4
  ♣ 6 3        S       ♣ K Q J 10 7
              ♠ Q 4 2
              ♥ J 6 5
              ♦ K Q J 9
              ♣ A 4 2
```

four Diamonds and the Aces of the other three suits. He had to create two more tricks, and he knew East had the Kings of the major suits. One extra trick he could make by throwing East in, and forcing him to lead from his Spades or his Hearts, provided East had only one Diamond. For the declarer could not afford to play more than one round of Diamonds. He had to preserve one of dummy's Diamonds as entry to the closed hand, and the other two of dummy's Diamonds would be needed to throw on East's Clubs, as dummys three Hearts and three Spades could not be touched. So from the start he had to assume a singleton Diamond with East. If East had two Diamonds, the contract could simply not be made.

First came the early throw-in and the gain of a trick from East's lead of Spades. Then came the squeeze for the gain of the second trick. And I set the whole complex process in operation by throwing East the lead in Clubs.

*　*　*

I was able to give the tiny black elf full meed of admiration for the delicacy with which his story had exploited the rare possibilities of the situation. The Queen of Hearts, too, delighted him by remarking she would have liked to see the Lecturer man trying to win his spurs by playing that dummy the right way.

Then the Club Three must needs mar the pleasure of his slightly elder brother by exclaiming jealously:

"I don't think Five's part in the play was so very important. Any low card of our tribe would have done. He might just as well have been marked in the diagram as an x. Not that I favour that, of course. Oh, Master Robert, if you knew how we lower inhabitants of the Pack detest writers who annihilate our identities by making their diagrams one mass of x's! One of the reasons why we humble folk hold you in such high esteem is that you never insult us by such slovenly and heartless conduct. Always in your diagrams we are given each of us his due place as a named and individual entity. How right you are in this I shall now demonstrate by telling you about a deal in which I and my young brother the Two could not possibly have been represented by x's. And so I shall choose as title for my story—"

A TREY WINS BY WEIGHT

(*The Tale of the Three of Clubs*)

SOUTH WAS PLAYING THE EVERY-DAY CONTRACT OF THREE
No-Trumps, and I was dealt to the West hand, thus:

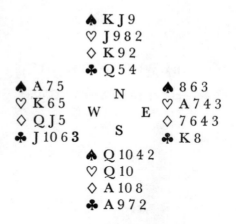

	♠ K J 9 ♡ J 9 8 2 ◇ K 9 2 ♣ Q 5 4	
♠ A 7 5 ♡ K 6 5 ◇ Q J 5 ♣ J 10 6 3	N W E S	♠ 8 6 3 ♡ A 7 4 3 ◇ 7 6 4 3 ♣ K 8
	♠ Q 10 4 2 ♡ Q 10 ◇ A 10 8 ♣ A 9 7 2	

My man, West, led the Knave of Clubs, the Queen, King, and Ace going on the first trick. The declarer led the Queen of Hearts, and East's Ace made. East returned the Eight of Clubs; South covered with the Nine; and my man's Ten took the trick. He led the Six of Clubs, dummy's Five dropping and South's Seven made. Later my man regained the lead, and cashed me for the setting trick, my brother, the Deuce, falling beneath my superior weight.

No x's could have represented the Club suit in that deal. Transpose me and my younger brother, and no defence can defeat the contract. I broke that contract in my own right as a master card of my tribe—not as a mere thirteenth. So closely balanced were the opposing strength, that the difference between victory and defeat was measured by the difference between me and the Deuce.

Perhaps it might be imagined the declarer could make his contract by ducking the first trick in dummy instead of covering with the Queen. Not so. East too, would duck, and

South's Ace would take the trick. When East got the lead with his Ace of Hearts, he would return a Diamond; and when my man, West, took a trick, he would pass the lead to East with a Club, and East would play another Diamond. This would enable West to defeat the contract with a Diamond trick as soon as he got in with his second entry.

So it all depended on which side had me and which my younger brother. At the end of the play North began to blame his partner, declaring that he (South) had not had sufficient strength to go Three No-Trumps. South replied, with a meekness that delighted his two opponents and the kibitzers:

"You are quite right. It was reckless overbidding on my part, as I had only the Deuce of Clubs instead of the Three. But I miserably failed to realise the importance of that. I should be most grateful if you would teach me the bidding system that would enable me to distinguish between the value of Ace-Nine-Seven-Three in a suit over Ace-Nine-Seven-Two."

*   *   *

This witticism rocked the Wee Folk with laughter. And certainly the Club Three had put it over rather well. Even the Club Five, I was happy to observe, had evidently forgotten how his exploit had been disparaged by the Trey, and joined in the mirth, proud of the success of his younger brother's story.

Then the Three of Spades stepped forward. At the moment the smaller cards undoubtedly had the floor.

"It may be rare," he said, "for us low-numbered denizens

123

of the Pack to exert a decisive degree of power; but it can happen, as you have just seen. What is more, it can happen in a freak deal just as well as in the evenly distributed hand the Club Three has told us of. In the adventure that is my most treasured memory—for in it I came into my own—the deal was indeed a freak, and the low cards of no fewer than two suits could not have had their individualities ignored by the x-mongers we small folk hate so heartily. It was a brilliantly subtle defence, in which I played an indispensable part as—"

A TREY THAT KILLED DUMMY

(The Tale of the Three of Spades)

AS YOU MAY IMAGINE, THERE WAS FORCEFUL BIDDING ON
this deal:

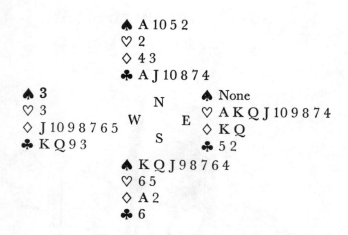

```
        ♠ A 10 5 2
        ♡ 2
        ◇ 4 3
        ♣ A J 10 8 7 4
♠ 3                        ♠ None
♡ 3           N            ♡ A K Q J 10 9 8 7 4
◇ J 10 9 8 7 6 5  W   E    ◇ K Q
♣ K Q 9 3     S            ♣ 5 2
        ♠ K Q J 9 8 7 6 4
        ♡ 6 5
        ◇ A 2
        ♣ 6
```

East bid his Hearts vigorously, but North-South were not to be denied, and South was eventually allowed to buy the contract at Six Spades. West led the Three of Hearts, and East's Seven took the trick. East pondered a few moments, and then made the superb return of the Four of Hearts. South had to head the trick with the Six; West ruffed with me; and this forced out dummy's Five of trumps.

All was now over for the declarer. He still had two entries in dummy with which to set up the Clubs, but he lacked the third entry to cash them—the entry which the Five of Spades would have afforded. There was no getting away from South's losing Diamond.

Was that not a beautiful defence? And observe the important part played by the differing values of the low Spades and low Hearts. Because East's Four of Hearts was lower than South's Six, West was made to ruff; and because I was one spot higher than my brother, the Deuce, North's Five of trumps had to go, and dummy was killed. Not a Single Club could be made except the Ace.

*   *   *

A round of shrill applause greeted the end of this bright little cameo. Before any of the high cards could speak, the Four of Clubs exclaimed:

"Now that's what I call bridge! None of your long-drawn-out exercises in reasoning and deduction and counting. Just one penetrating *apercu,* a brilliant decision, and— pouf! the unbreakable contract is broken. That is bridge at its best."

The goblin looked around with a grin that broadened into a chuckle.

"I emphasise my tribute to the swift insight of opportunism because the story I have to tell is the reverse—a veritable tour-de-force of analytical logic. But don't look so apprehensive, Master Robert. You won't be bored. I promise you something unusual, something pleasingly intricate, but not difficult to dullness—indeed, not really difficult at all. In fact, it may be described as—"

ELEMENTARY, MY DEAR WATSON

(*The Tale of the Four of Clubs*)

PARTNERSHIP EVENING AT THE CLUB WAS DRAWING TO its close, and some players had already gone home. The last rubber at my table had just ended. The stakes had been paid, and the four men had risen and moved from the table. They were standing a few yards away, still chatting, when there came from the other side of the room two men, who were also evidently on the point of leaving. One was tall, thin, and wiry, with aquiline features. The other was shorter, stoutish, thickset, and his rounded face was slightly rubicund.

The short man was leading, and he walked to the right of my table, on which lay the pack of cards that had been used in the final deal. I happened to be on the top of the pack, and so saw and heard all. The short man, walking to the right, passed between the table and the group of four who had played there. The tall man walked to the left of the table, and as he went by, he deftly seized the pack on which I was lying, and put another pack in its place.

The next thing I knew, we were in a taxi. As he got in, I heard the tall man give the driver an address in Baker Street. The tall man drew the pack out of his pocket and held it toward the short man.

"I have it, Watson," he said, in a tone of quiet triumph. "You did what I asked you very neatly. At the moment I took this pack from the table and substituted another, you were screening me beautifully from the four men. I'll wager they did not notice a thing."

He lifted the top card carefully from the pack, and looked at me; he then glanced at the bottom card.

"The Four of Clubs at the top," he said, "and the King of Spades at the bottom. In those cards and the fifty between them lies, I hope, the solution of my problem and the fate of a criminal. Since I sent for you to partner me at the club this evening, Watson, I haven't had time to explain matters to you. Nor have I time now for detailed narration. I must work quickly. For the moment let it suffice for you to know that it is vital I should discover whether the man who played the final hand as declarer

130

with these cards to-night is or is not an expert bridge player. If he is, my case is complete; I shall place my information in the hands of Scotland Yard; and the late editions of to-morrow morning's newspapers will contain the story of a sensational arrest. If not—well, I shall have to begin my investigations anew."

"But how on earth will you be able to tell how the declarer played from that pack of cards?" asked the other.

"I do not expect any great difficulty," said the tall man, nonchalantly. "For fear of arousing the man's suspicions I did not dare approach his table while he played, for he knows me by sight. Nor could I question members of the club about him, for he is not himself a member. I learned by a piece of good luck that he was playing there as a guest to-night. So I saw the Club Secretary, explained matters to him, and obtained permission for you and me to play there too. I watched my quarry from across the room, and when I saw he had just finished the rubber, and had played the last hand as declarer, I knew fortune was once more with me. We have only to analyse the cards in this pack, deduce how the play went, and what was the contract, to discover, I trust whether or not the declarer played like an expert. We shall soon know now, Watson, for here we are at our diggings."

A few minutes later the two men, with drinks at their elbows, were leaning over a round table in the middle of a comfortably furnished sitting room. With a large, well-smoked pipe between his teeth, the tall man took in his hand the pack of cards, with me still lying on the top of it. He faced it, and dealt the cards face upward across the table in rows. As he did so, he said:

"We shall find all the cards in their proper order inside each trick, I believe, Watson, for I noticed that both sides kept their tricks neatly stacked. But we shall not know the exact order of the tricks. One of the players pushed the declarer's tricks together and did the same with the defence's tricks, and then placed the one pile on top of the other. So one of the things we must find out is the order of the tricks. We should have little difficulty in deciding what is the trump suit, if any. We know the declarer made his contract, for this hand ended the rubber; but we must deduce what the contract was; and by that time we should be able to say whether the hand was played well or badly by the declarer. Let us hope it was not too straightforward a deal to be revealing."

By this time he had set out the fifty-two cards in rows, thus:

♠ K	♠ 7	♠ 5	♠ 4	♡ 7	♡ 3	♡ A	♡ K	◇ 7
◇ 6	♡ 4	◇ A	◇ 8	♣ 3	♡ 6	◇ K	♠ 3	♠ 2
♠ A	♠ 6	♡ 9	♡ 2	♡ 8	♡ Q	♡ 10	♡ 5	♣ 7
♡ J	♠ 9	◇ 3	♠ Q	♠ 10	♠ 8	♣ 8	♠ J	◇ 4
♣ 9	♣ J	♣ 2	◇ 9	♣ 10	♣ K	♣ Q	◇ 5	◇ Q
◇ J	◇ 10	◇ 2	♣ 5	♣ 6	♣ A	♣ 4		

"Good heavens, Holmes," exclaimed Dr. Watson, "how are you going to get any sense or meaning out of that conglomeration?"

"Well," returned Holmes, equably, "I think we'll have to alter the order of the cards a bit. You see, by beginning with the bottom card of the pack we have placed first the last card played to each trick. The card led was the fourth card in each trick as we have placed them, and the third card was played by second player, and so on. So now let us reverse the order in each group of four cards, placing the fourth card first, the third card second, and so on. Then we shall have the cards in their order of play inside each trick. While I am thus rearranging the cards, do you, my dear fellow, tear a piece of notepaper into thirteen portions, and we will give each trick a letter of the alphabet for easy reference."

The two men worked in silence for a few moments, and then the cards on the table were spread out in tricks like this:

(a)	♠ 4	♠ 5	♠ 7	♠ K
(b)	♥ K	♥ A	♥ 3	♥ 7
(c)	♦ A	♥ 4	♦ 6	♦ 7
(d)	♦ K	♥ 6	♣ 3	♦ 8
(e)	♠ 6	♠ A	♠ 2	♠ 3
(f)	♥ Q	♥ 8	♥ 2	♥ 9
(g)	♥ J	♣ 7	♥ 5	♥ 10
(h)	♠ 10	♠ Q	♦ 3	♠ 9
(i)	♦ 4	♠ J	♣ 8	♠ 8
(k)	♦ 9	♣ 2	♣ J	♣ 9
(l)	♦ 5	♣ Q	♣ K	♣ 10
(m)	♦ 2	♦ 10	♦ J	♦ Q
(n)	♣ 4	♣ A	♣ 6	♣ 5

"That looks more lifelike," pronounced Sherlock Holmes, with satisfaction. "The first card of each trick is now the

(a)	♣ 4	♣ 5	♣ 7	♠ K
(b)	♡ K	♡ A	♡ 3	♡ 7
(c)	◇ A	♡ 4	◇ 6	◇ 7
(d)	◇ K	♡ 6	♣ 3	◇ 8
(e)	♠ 6	♠ A	♠ 2	♠ 3
(f)	♡ Q	♡ 8	♡ 2	♡ 9
(g)	♡ J	♣ 7	♡ 5	♡ 10
(h)	♠ 10	♠ Q	◇ 3	♠ 9
(i)	◇ 4	♠ J	♣ 8	♠ 8
(k)	◇ 9	♣ 2	♣ J	♣ 9
(l)	◇ 5	♣ Q	♣ K	♣ 10
(m)	◇ 2	◇ 10	◇ J	◇ Q
(n)	♣ 4	♣ A	♣ 6	♣ 5

card that was led; the second card is that played by the opponent on the leader's left: the third card is that played by the leader's partner—and so on. It therefore follows that if a trick is taken by the first card or the third card, the lead remains with the side that had the lead; while if a trick is taken by the second or fourth card, it means the lead was captured by the other side from the side that had the lead. In that way we can tell in each trick whether the lead remained with the side that had it or whether it passed in that trick from one side to the other. And now what can we make of it all? Let us begin at the bottom. Do you observe tricks (m) and (n), Watson? One is an all-Diamond trick and the other all Clubs. But they are preceded by trick (l) in which a Diamond is led and all the other players throw Clubs. What does that convey to you?"

"It's sheer nonsense, Holmes. You cannot have three players failing to follow to Diamonds in one trick, and in the next trick all of them playing Diamonds."

"Excellent, my dear Watson. Of course, it is nonsense, Therefore it did not happen. Trick (m) was not subsequent to trick (l), but must have been played earlier. In other words, trick (m) was not taken by the same side that took trick (l). That is, trick (m) was taken by the defence. So, you may be sure was trick (n). Note that the fourth card

134

in trick (m) took the trick, and the second card in trick (n) That shows both were tricks captured from the side that had the lead. You remember the contract was made, as it ended the rubber. Therefore the declarer made the majority of the tricks. You also remember the declarer's tricks and the defence's tricks were placed on top of each other in two piles. So I think it is clear that tricks (m) and (n) were taken by the defence and all the rest, tricks (a) to (l), were the declarer's."

"Wonderful, Holmes."

"Elementary, my dear Watson. And now we must find where these defence tricks fit in. I think you will agree, my dear fellow, that if these are the only tricks taken by the defence, and if both were captured from the side which had the lead, we may assume that the first trick, (a), was taken by the declarer. If we call the declarer, as usual, South, West led the Four of Spades, and South's King won."

"Yes, I agree that must be so."

"In that case, trick (b) could not have been the second trick of the play."

"I'm afraid I do not follow you Holmes."

"Tut, tut, Watson. Look more closely at the trick. You know my methods. Do you not notice that the highest card is the second played to the trick. What does that mean?"

"That it was taken from the side that had the lead."

"Good, Watson. Exactly. Therefore as the declarer had won the lead in trick (a), and also took trick (b), which was taken from the side which had the lead, there must have been some other trick between trick (*a*) and trick (*b*) This is obviously trick (*m*), in which the trick was taken from the side which had the lead—the declarer's side—by East's Queen of Diamonds. Therefore, it was East who led the King of Hearts in trick (*b*), South taking the trick with his Ace. Is that clear?"

"It is marvellous, Holmes."

"A quite simple deduction, I think, my dear fellow. To proceed. In tricks (*c*) and (*d*) the lead remained with the declarer. That is obvious, the highest card in each case being the first. But in trick (*e*) you again notice that the second card is the highest. Therefore, according to our previous reasoning, trick (e) did not come immediately after trick (*d*). The second defence trick—trick (*n*)—came in here. West won the trick with the Ace of Clubs, and led the Six of Spades in trick (*e*). From now on tricks (*f*), (*g*), (*h*), (*i*), (*k*) and (*l*) went to the declarer's side. And, of course, Diamonds were trumps."

"Are you sure, Holmes? I was beginning to think the hand was played in No-Trumps. I can't see any trumping."

"Look at trick (*h*), Watson. The lead is with the declarer's side, and a Spade is led. Second player puts on the highest Spade in the trick, and yet the declarer's side won the trick, as we know. Obviously, the trick was won by ruffing with the Diamond Three."

"Yes, I see that now. And I suppose that as the declarer made eleven tricks in Diamonds, and the defence only two, the contract was Five Diamonds, made. But I don't see how you will tell from all this whether South was an expert or not."

"Not so fast, my dear fellow. As we now know the exact order of the tricks, we can reconstruct the whole deal, and follow the play. This is how the cards were distributed:

```
                    ♠ A 10 5
                    ♡ Q J 7
                    ◇ J 6
                    ♣ K J 8 6 3
    ♠ J 9 6 4          N          ♠ Q 8 7 2
    ♡ 10 9 6 4 3                  ♡ K 8
    ◇ 10         W         E      ◇ Q 8 7
    ♣ A Q 2          S           ♣ 10 9 7 5
                    ♠ K 3
                    ♡ A 5 2
                    ◇ A K 9 5 4 3 2
                    ♣ 4
```

"The play," continued Sherlock Holmes, "was as follows: West led the Spade Four, and South's King took trick (a). South led the Two of Diamonds to the table's Knave, and East's Queen made, trick (m). East returned the King of Hearts, which fell to South's Ace, trick (b). South drew trumps with the Ace and King of Diamonds. tricks (c) and (d). Then he led the Four of Clubs, which West took with the Ace, trick (n). West led a Spade, which dummy's Ace took, trick (e), and dummy cashed his Queen and Knave of Hearts, tricks (f) and (g). Dummy's last Spade was ruffed by South, trick (h), and South made the

137

```
            ♠ A 10 5
            ♥ Q J 7
            ♦ J 6
            ♣ K J 8 6 3
♠ J 9 6 4       N        ♠ Q 8 7 2
♥ 10 9 6 4 3             ♥ K 8
♦ 10        W       E    ♦ Q 8 7
♣ A Q 2         S        ♣ 10 9 7 5
            ♠ K 3
            ♥ A 5 2
            ♦ A K 9 5 4 3 2
            ♣ 4
```

last three tricks with trumps, tricks (*i*), (*k*) and (*l*). And so I have my man, Watson. South's play was certainly expert."

"What do you mean, Holmes?"

"Did you not notice his fine lead of the Two of trumps at the second trick, my dear fellow? That was a first-rate safety play to guard against losing more than one trick in the suit, if the adverse distribution should be 4-0. If West has all four trumps, he could make only the Queen because of the good position of the Knave in dummy. If East has all four, West would show out on the first round, and then the declarer could play trumps from dummy and finesse against East's Ten. Yes, South is my man all right. I'll just let Lestrade know he can arrest him at once."

So saying, Sherlock Holmes rose from the table and went towards the telephone on the mantelpiece. He was just about to dial a number, when he turned towards Dr. Watson.

"By the way, my dear fellow," he said, "you were wrong in thinking the contract was Five Diamonds. It can only have been Four Diamonds and nothing else. In Five Diamonds the safety play would have been sheer folly. It would have imperilled the contract, as there might be a losing Heart. And if the contract had been Three Diamonds, the safety play was unnecessary, as then South could have afforded to lose two trump tricks. The only reason why he did in fact make eleven tricks was East's desperate effort to break the contract by leading his King of Hearts at the third trick. No, the contract was Four Diamonds."

"Holmes," exclaimed Dr. Watson, "that really is marvellous."

Sherlock Holmes smiled a small smile of vanity.

"Well," he said, "perhaps that bit was not quite so elementary. And now to unleash Lestrade."

He turned to the telephone, and from the table where I still lay in South's hand, I watched, fascinated, as Sherlock Holmes dialled:

"W H I 1212."

* * *

The reaction of the Little People to the story was surprising. They may, of course, have been as impressed as I was by the famous detective's unerring reconstruction of the deal and play, but they gave no sign of that. Instead, they assailed the Club Four with questions.

"What happened next?"

"Was there a sensational arrest next morning?"

"Who was the criminal? and what had he done—murder?"

"Was he convicted and hanged?"

"Surely Holmes told the whole story to Dr. Watson that night after he had rung Scotland Yard. Didn't you hear it?"

"What had bridge to do with the crime?"

The goblin looked bewildered, and then rather ashamed, as he confessed that he did not know, for certain, anything more.

"When Sherlock Holmes had finshed telephoning," he explained, "he slipped the pack, including me, of course, into a drawer of the table, and I could only hear the drone of their voices as the two men talked. Next morning Dr. Watson returned the pack to the club. All I can tell you is that when the Club Secretary received it he said: "To think this pack of cards has held a human life in balance! Curious, too, how many criminals confess when they are caught."

With his gnomish grin, the Club Four added:

"Deduce what you can from that. You know Holmes's methods."

"How extremely unsatisfactory!" exclaimed the Queen of Spades. And in the severity of her tone it was evident that she expressed the feeling of them all.

The Club Four once more looked abashed, and a silence fell. By this time, of course, I had come to realise that each one of the fifty-two denizens of the Pack was going to tell a tale. I looked curiously around to see who was to be next. The Queen of Clubs, a dark-eyed, quaintly pretty little person caught my eye. She smiled shyly, and said:

"The smaller folk, mainly from my own tribe, have been airing their contention that they, like the rest of us, may have value in play as individuals of intrinsic worth. As the consort of a thoroughly constitutional monarch, I should be the last to deny the truth of that. But it is also

140

true that we folk of high rank often maintain our importance in virtue of that rank even when we seem to function as mere units of our tribe. I am thinking of a deal where I had no hope of either taking a trick or promoting one of my tribe to trick-taking value. I was as completely a loser as if I had been an x, instead of a royal personage. And yet my Queenly rank had crucial worth. Without it, I should still have been a loser: but without it, I should not have been—"

A LOSER THAT PLACED THE LEAD

(The Tale of the Queen of Clubs)

THE BIDDING WAS EXCITING WHEN EAST, VULNERABLE
against non-vulnerable opponents, dealt these hands-:

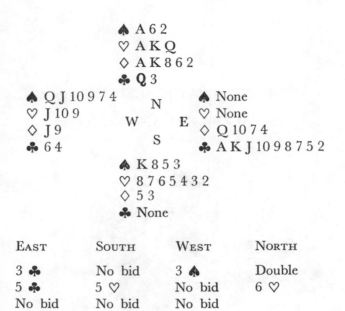

$\spadesuit$ A 6 2
$\heartsuit$ A K Q
$\diamondsuit$ A K 8 6 2
$\clubsuit$ Q 3

$\spadesuit$ Q J 10 9 7 4
$\heartsuit$ J 10 9
$\diamondsuit$ J 9
$\clubsuit$ 6 4

$\spadesuit$ None
$\heartsuit$ None
$\diamondsuit$ Q 10 7 4
$\clubsuit$ A K J 10 9 8 7 5 2

$\spadesuit$ K 8 5 3
$\heartsuit$ 8 7 6 5 4 3 2
$\diamondsuit$ 5 3
$\clubsuit$ None

EAST	SOUTH	WEST	NORTH
3 $\clubsuit$	No bid	3 $\spadesuit$	Double
5 $\clubsuit$	5 $\heartsuit$	No bid	6 $\heartsuit$
No bid	No bid	No bid	

West led the Queen of Spades. A low card was played from dummy; East threw the Knave of Clubs; and South's King won. Declarer played a trump to the table's Queen, West throwing the Nine, and East discarding the Deuce of Clubs. With the knowledge that East had no Spades and no Hearts, the declarer paused to sum up his chances.

He had seven Heart winners, two Spades, and two Diamonds—eleven in all. The twelfth trick could not be made by ruffing a Spade in dummy, for that would lose a trump trick. Clearly, the only hope was to do something with the Diamonds. Here a 5-1 split would render the contract unmakeable. Only East could hold the five Diamonds, and as he would discard after dummy, no squeeze of East

144

in Diamonds and Clubs was possible. If the Diamonds split
3-3, or if West had four Diamonds, the contract was easy to
make. To gamble on that, however, would be fatuous. It
was more likely that East had four Diamonds. The declarer
decided to address himself to that problem. He realised it
was a question of entries. If he drew trumps before ruffing
Diamonds, there would be no entry in dummy to cash the
thirteenth Diamond. Well, what about drawing trumps and
then allowing the defenders to take a Diamond trick before ruffing? That would be no good, he decided. West
might take the trick, and his Spade return would again
kill dummy. Clearly, then, the declarer could not afford to
draw trumps. The ideal thing, of course, would be to ruff a
Diamond early, before West could overruff. That seemed
impossible, as both South and West had two Diamonds
each.

But was it impossible? Suddenly, he saw the way out
of his difficulties. He leaned across to dummy, and led me.
West played the King of Clubs, and South discarded a
Diamond. Now he could ruff a Diamond while West still
held one.

The rest of the play was simple. Having no Spade with
which to attack the table's entry, East led a Club. South
ruffed; cashed the Ace of Diamonds; ruffed a Diamond;
drew two rounds of trumps, exhausting West; ruffed
another Diamond; and returned to the table with the precious Ace of Spades. Now the King of Diamonds and dummy's last Diamonds were played, on which South's two
losing Spades were thrown.

A prettily played hand, Master Robert, wasn't it? I filled

```
                ♠ A 6 2
                ♡ A K Q
                ♢ A K 8 6 2
                ♣ Q 3
♠ Q J 10 9 7 4          N          ♠ None
♡ J 10 9          W         E      ♡ None
♢ J 9                   S          ♢ Q 10 7 4
♣ 6 4                              ♣ A K J 10 9 8 7 5 2
                ♠ K 8 5 3
                ♡ 8 7 6 5 4 3 2
                ♢ 5 3
                ♣ None
```

a dual role. As a loser I functioned simply as a vehicle for the discard of a Diamond by South to reduce his Diamonds to one fewer than West's. But as Queen I ensured that the lead should be placed with East, who could not harm dummy's Spade entry. You note the declarer did not play the Three of Clubs instead of me. The Trey would have served just as well for the Diamond discard, but East would have been given the opportunity of playing the Five of Clubs, trusting to West to have the Six, as indeed he did have. West would then have led a Spade, and broken the contract. Unlikely for East, perhaps; but by leading me and not the trey the declarer made a certainty of placing the lead where he wanted it.

The honours looked pleased at this defence of their status, but the rest, it was apparent, were too inured to the nobility's assertion of superiority either to resent or accept it. The Nine of Diamonds epitomised the situation when he said, lightly:

"Intermediate between high and low, I find this never-ending quarrel about playing values as barren as you doubtless do, Master Robert. After all, any citizen of the Pack who does a good job of work, scores for his side, and that is all that matters."

"You're quite right," put in the Seven of Spades. "But

146

I don't suppose Master Robert minds our puny arguments as long as they continue to result in hands remarkable enough to entertain him. To get on to something with more substance to it, did you notice, Master Robert, that two out of the last three deals contained suits of nine cards? And have you observed that nine, or possibly ten, cards seem to constitute the practical limit of strength? I mean, one practically never comes across a hand of any real playing interest with eleven or twelve cards to a suit. I don't know why that should be, but so it is. One has to jump from nine or ten of a suit to the complete single-suited hand to find a tale worth telling. Even then it is generally only the bidding that is of consequence. But I remember once being concerned in a highly diverting piece of play that followed on some amazing bidding when one of the players had—"

THIRTEEN OF A SUIT

(The Tale of the Seven of Spades)

WITH BOTH SIDES VULNERABLE, SOUTH DEALT THIS
colossal freak:

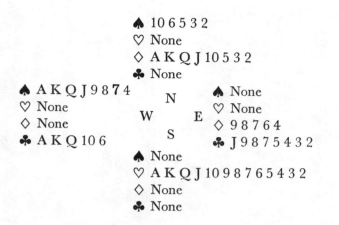

♠ 10 6 5 3 2
♡ None
◇ A K Q J 10 5 3 2
♣ None

♠ A K Q J 9 8 7 4   N   ♠ None
♡ None   ♡ None
◇ None   W   E   ◇ 9 8 7 6 4
♣ A K Q 10 6   S   ♣ J 9 8 7 5 4 3 2

♠ None
♡ A K Q J 10 9 8 7 6 5 4 3 2
◇ None
♣ None

South was notorious as an inveterate psychic bidder, but as I had been dealt to the West hand, I cannot tell you from my own knowledge what was his motive in deciding to open with a bid of Two Spades. I can, however, relate the thoughts that passed through West's mind. He knew South's reputation, and was himself a particularly astute and discerning player. When I heard South's astonishing call, I looked deep into West's eyes to follow what he was thinking.

"So South's at it again with his psychs, is he?" my man was saying to himself. "But this is a particularly outrageous one. He must be terrified of Spades. Now why? Well, I suppose he has a terrific lot of Hearts or Diamonds or both. It doesn't matter which. It doesn't even matter if he has all thirteen of either, because I'm going to make it plumb impossible for him to make another bid. Obviously, as he has chosen not to mention his real suit, I, on my glorious hand, must shut him out—and if I'm going to shut him out, I may as well do it completely. It's perfectly safe for me to do as I like, because I can always go into Spades if I'm doubled. Here goes!"

And in a firm voice, West said:

"Seven Hearts."

I glanced at South, and saw him go white. Then he recovered himself, and looked with pitiable hope across at his partner. But North had no reason to hesitate long. In an equally firm voice, he made his bid.

"Seven Spades."

East passed, and I saw South sway in his chair. He said the only thing he could: "No bid," and his voice cracked as he said it. North merely thought that piteous sound excitement; and when West doubled remorselessly, North eagerly redoubled. South could still do nothing but pass.

West, knowing all the missing Spades must be with North, cunningly led me. South was anxious not to lose control of trumps immediately, as he hoped he might yet do something with the Diamond suit; so he played low in dummy, and I held the trick. West now drew all North's trumps, and not a single trick could the declarer make. A thirteen-trick defeat, vulnerable, with the defense scoring four honors to boot, represented a loss of 7,700 points. This I believe to be an all-time record.

South was so abjectly miserable that North, to his credit, said little. South explained that he had remembered the famous Vanderbilt hand, where a bid of Seven Spades, based on thirteen of the suit, was overcalled by the next player with Seven No-Trumps, which was made.

"I wanted to avoid that happening," said South "and so I decided to bluff first with Two of one of the other suits."

"But what in Hades made you choose a higher-ranking suit which you could not outbid?" asked North.

"That's just what I don't know," moaned South.

* * *

"Poor man!" said the Queen of Diamonds, in a soft, low voice. "I suppose every bridge player has thought and thought about what he would or should do if he found himself holding an entire suit. But when the miracle happens, it must be so thrilling that it is no wonder if judgment and self-possession go overboard."

"You speak of miracles, Mam," said the Ace of Hearts, "applying the term, with pardonable hyperbole, to what is, though a great rarity, in the natural order of things. But what would your Majesty say if I told you of a hand in which the Ace of trumps failed to take a trick. Would you not more fitly call that a miracle?"

"Don't be silly," the Diamond Queen replied, her smile and sweet voice making the words gentle raillery.

"Oh, it happened all right," insisted the Ace of Hearts, "though it was a long time ago. In 1930, to be exact. It might amuse you all to hear about it. There is, I assure you, Master Robert, a bridge player alive today who remembers—"

GOING TO BED WITH THE ACE OF TRUMPS

(*The Tale of the Ace of Hearts*)

SLAM BIDDING IN 1930 WAS NOT WHAT IT IS TO-DAY. BUT
even for those far-off times North-South might be accounted
a trifle venturesome in reaching a contract of Seven Hearts
with the deal as follows:

153

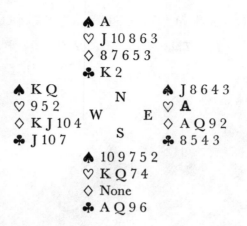

```
              ♠ A
              ♡ J 10 8 6 3
              ◇ 8 7 6 5 3
              ♣ K 2
  ♠ K Q           N        ♠ J 8 6 4 3
  ♡ 9 5 2                  ♡ A
  ◇ K J 10 4   W    E      ◇ A Q 9 2
  ♣ J 10 7        S        ♣ 8 5 4 3
              ♠ 10 9 7 5 2
              ♡ K Q 7 4
              ◇ None
              ♣ A Q 9 6
```

All four players had some good cards, and North-South had bid cleverly enough to discover what excellent distribution they had. The one flaw in their contract was that they failed either of them to hold me, the Ace of trumps. East doubled, and grinned happily as he looked at me in his hand.

West led the King of Spades, and when North tabled his cards, the declarer exclaimed disgustedly:

"One down. I must lose a trick to the Ace of trumps."

"No," said West, who had hoped to make a trick or two himself, "please play the hand out."

Grumblingly, South complied. Making the first trick with dummy's Ace of Spades, he cashed the Ace, King, and Queen of Clubs, discarding a Diamond from dummy on the third Club. Then he ruffed a Club in dummy; ruffed a Diamond in his own hand; ruffed a Spade in dummy; ruffed another Diamond in his hand; ruffed another Spade in dummy; ruffed a third Diamond in his hand; and led a third Spade from his hand to the eleventh trick, when West suddenly exclaimed:

"I've only two cards left, and dummy has three."

East counted his cards, and said:

"Good gracious! I have four cards."

"Thank heavens for that!" ejaculated South. "It's a misdeal. The hand is wiped out, and there must be a fresh deal."

"Just a moment," said West. "I believe there's a rule to cover this."

A copy of the Laws was sent for, and there it was found that if both hands of either partnership had an incorrect number of cards, there had to be a fresh deal, provided the discrepancy was discovered before the ninth trick was turned. If it was discovered only in a later trick, the deal had to stand and be played to the end with the cards just as they were.

South therefore had to go on with the play. He continued the cross-ruff for the last three cards in his hand and the last three in dummy; and to his astonishment and joy, East was able to follow suit each time. So the declarer made all thirteen tricks, and East was left at the end, staring at me, solitary in his hand, with no trick to play me to.

"Good lord!" he said, dazedly. "This has never happened to anyone else in the world. I have gone to bed with the Ace of trumps!"

I may add that in 1932 the Laws were revised, and since then a fresh deal has been ordained whenever two or more hands are found to have an incorrect number of cards at any stage of the play. So my curious experience can never be repeated.

*   *   *

Amid the chuckles this queer tale drew from the crowd of small creatures the Queen of Diamonds smiled her charming smile across at the Heart Ace.

"I told you not to be silly," she said; "and I suppose you have disobeyed me, as that is really a very silly story. Still, it is certainly an historical curiosity worth being placed on record. But I shouldn't say it was a miracle. Now I once did perform a miracle. Or shall we call it something less pretentious—a tiny piece of magic? It was one of the rare occasions when I decided to play the part of—"

A FAIRY GODMOTHER

(*The Tale of the Queen of Diamonds*)

IT IS ONLY TO A VERY FEW FAVOURED MORTALS THAT WE
People of the Pack ever make known our existence. This

man was decidedly a favourite of mine. Not only was he a fine bridge player, but he had a delightful way with him, and was always the soul of courtesy and consideration. He had acquired merit in my eyes by deeds of kindness at the bridge table, most of which passed unnoticed and unacknowledged. For instance, I have seen him deliberately refrain from drawing attention to an opponent's harmless revoke that did not affect the course of play. How many people ever do that? I have known him intervene tactfully as peacemaker between quarrelling partners; and I have never known him quarrel with his own partner.

So when Brigidda, the goddess of bridge—who, I sometimes think, is more of a witch than a goddess—inflicted on him an unusually long period of bad luck, I felt full of pity for him. He bore the hazards of misfortune so well and cheerfully. He did not moan about it. He did not dispirit his partner by remarking when they cut together: "Don't expect me to do anything, partner. I haven't held any cards for days." Nor did he get impatient at his run of ill luck, and let his partner down by gross overbidding when he did happen to have a few honours.

There came a session that tried even his fortitude. That afternoon Brigidda had vouchsafed him a reasonable number of biddable hands. But with malicious intent. Throughout the afternoon he failed in contract after contract, and I've said he was a fine player. Voids and singletons kept cropping up in his opponents' hands, trumps seemed always massed against him, and side-outs obstinately refused to allow themselves to be set up.

158

At the end of the session, when the rest of the players had gone home or were treating each other in the bar to before-dinner cocktails, he threw himself dejectedly into an armchair by the bridge room fire, and muttered:

"Hal Sims says one ought to take advantage of a time of ill-luck to become fifty per cent better at defensive play than one was before. But he doesn't say what one should do as a declarer whose every contract is doomed by incredibly adverse distributions. If one is not to bid when one has the cards, what the devil is one to do?"

It was at this moment that I arose from out of a pack on a near-by table and addressed him:

"Be not so sad," I said. "Behold! I have come to bring you solace and, if I can, a change of fortune."

I had used a bit of magic to give myself an airy effulgence, so that I was bathed in a faint rosy glow. And the flower I held in my hand I waved in mystic movement like an enchanted wand.

He stared for a moment in amazement.

"Who are you?" he stammered. "O Vision of Beauty, who are you?"

"I am your fairy godmother—at any rate at the bridge table."

"At the bridge table?" he echoed, questioningly. "I thought there was something familiar in all that radiance. And now I see who you are. None other than Her Majesty the Queen of Diamonds."

He rose from his chair, and bowed before me.

"Yes," I confirmed, "I am the Diamond Queen, but also your bridge fairy godmother. I have noted your kindly behaviour to partners and opponents alike. You are that rarity—a chivalrous bridge player. And now I have come to bring you your reward. Sit down at this table, and consider the hand I shall give you to play. It is a test. If you pass it, your bad luck will change to good. You have suffered, have you not from excessively uneven distributions of the opposing cards. Well, ponder on that hint, which is all I may give you, and consider this hand."

In a daze, he moved over to my table, and sat down at it. I had awaiting him these cards:

♠ A 8 7 5 2
♡ A K 2
◇ Q 5 2
♣ A 2

                N
        W   E
                S

♠ 3
♡ Q 10 8 6
◇ A 10 8 6 3
♣ 6 4 3

"Here is the test," I told him. "Hearts are trumps. You can choose whether West should make the opening lead

160

from a black suit or from a red. Moreover, you can arrange the distribution of your opponents' cards as you like. Make them up what hands you will. The question I put to you is two-fold: What Heart contract do you undertake to fulfill with those conditions, and how would you play the hand? Think well."

And I smiled encouragingly at him.

"I obey your will, O Beautious Queen and most potent Godmother," he replied, and set himself to his task.

There were a few moments silence, and then I heard him murmur under his breath:

"If I give the King of Diamonds to West, I can make four Diamonds, four Hearts, and two black Aces. That's game. But wait a minute. I can do better than that. Suppose I give West the singleton Knave of Diamonds—as if I hadn't had enough of singletons in opponents' hands this afternoon!—then I could make five Diamond tricks, and with a Club ruff—"

He lapsed into silence. Then suddenly spoke aloud in firm, ringing tones:

"O Fairy Godmother, I now understand this hand and your sweetly benevolent intentions. I am to realise that freakish distributions in opponents' hands may as well work for as against the declarer. It is a true lesson, and I shall profit by it. With a 6-0 split in trumps and arranged like this, I guarantee to make the Grand Slam in Hearts."

He quickly laid out the complete deal.

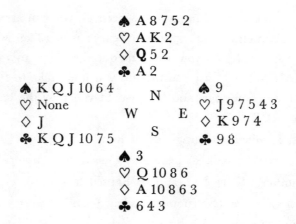

♠ A 8 7 5 2
♡ A K 2
◇ **Q** 5 2
♣ A 2

♠ K Q J 10 6 4
♡ None
◇ J
♣ K Q J 10 7 5

N W E S

♠ 9
♡ J 9 7 5 4 3
◇ K 9 7 4
♣ 9 8

♠ 3
♡ Q 10 8 6
◇ A 10 8 6 3
♣ 6 4 3

"I choose that West lead from a red suit," said my now jubilant protege. "So he has to begin with the Knave of Diamonds. The first card I play from dummy is thine image, dearest of godmothers. East covers, but it makes no difference if he doesn't. South's Ace takes. I cross to the table with the Ace of Clubs, and finesse Diamonds. Back I go to dummy with the Ace of Spades, and take the second Diamond finesse. Now I cash South's high Diamond, discarding dummy's losing Club, and ruff a Club in dummy. I then make the remaining six tricks with cross-ruffs.

"Although East has six trumps, he cannot take a single trick. The 6-0 division of trumps is the only way all thirteen tricks can be made, for South must make four Diamond tricks, and this is possible only if West has no trumps at all. The declarer must never lead a trump. All his seven trumps must be made separately. Then he can make seven trump tricks, four Diamonds, and the two black Aces."

"Well spoken!" I said. "You have passed the test, and

proved yourself worthy of favourable distributions. Now all will be well with you. Farewell."

And before he could do more than utter a responding "Farewell" I had vanished back into the pack that lay on the table.

That night after dinner he entered the bridge room, as I had intended he should, heartened and with renewed zest. And, strange to relate, his luck had turned, and he won, and won handsomely.

The Wee Folk clapped their hands with pleasure at the happy outcome of the Diamond Queen's "tiny piece of magic." All but the King of Spades.

* * *

"The last three or four tales," he said severely, "have been frivolous to a degree. If we go on like this, Master Robert will think we are more attracted by the bizarre than by the sterling worth of straightforward good bridge. An occasional oddity is all very well, but we don't want Master Robert to imagine he has fallen in with a bridge edition of the B.B.C.'s Puzzle Corner. I think it high time someone recalled an honest-to-goodness hand with honest-to-goodness bidding and play."

There was a moment's rather abashed silence, and then the Six of Hearts stepped forward.

"I was once the critical card in just such a hand," he said. "What is more, there was good defence as well as good dummy play; while the bidding, too, was of importance. I think the hand can best be described as—"

A LESSON IN RUFFING

(*The Tale of the Six of Hearts*)

ONCE THE BIDDING WAS OVER, IT WAS A CONTEST BETWEEN
the declarer and East, both of whom were excellent players.
Here are the hands and the auction:

♠ 9 6
♡ K Q 6 4 2
◇ J 6 4 2
♣ Q 3

♠ J 10 7 4 3   ♠ 8 5
♡ 7   ♡ J 10 9 8
◇ A Q 9 8 7 3   ◇ K 10 5
♣ 4   ♣ K 10 8 7

N
W   E
S

♠ A K Q 2
♡ A 5 3
◇ None
♣ A J 9 6 5 2

SOUTH	WEST	NORTH	EAST
1 ♣	1 ◇	1 ♡	1 N-T
2 ◇	No bid	2 ♡	3 ◇
4 ♠	Double	5 ♣	No bid
6 ♣	No bid	No bid	Double
No bid	No bid	No bid	

West led the Seven of Hearts. The bidding had given
the declarer a fairly good idea of the distribution against
him. West, who had bid Diamonds and doubled Spades,
must be credited with five or six of each suit. East's No-
Trumps over Clubs and Hearts and his Club double marked
him with four Hearts to the Knave and four Clubs to the
King-Ten. Obviously, then, the Heart lead was a singleton,
and West could not hold more than a single Club.

Dummy's Queen of Hearts took the first trick. The
declarer then decided that West's lone trump must be re-
moved lest it interfere with later manoeuvres. So the Three
of Clubs was led from dummy, and South's Nine was

166

finessed. It would have been a mistake to play the Queen of Clubs. She was needed for more important work to ruff South's Two of Spades in order to tempt East to overruff and so weaken his trump holding, for, clearly, the declarer was threatened with the loss of two trump tricks. But suppose East declined to overruff? There would then be no trump in dummy to lead through East. The difficulty could be met only by a trump end-play. But there was a dangerous superfluous card in South's hand—one of the high Spades. That must be got rid of, and the only parking place for it was dummy's fifth Heart. Therefore, the first task must be to establish that card.

So the declarer played out the Ace and King of Hearts and ruffed the Four of Hearts, leaving me in dummy as the master thirteenth. The Ace and King of Spades were cashed, and then South led the Deuce of Spades, and ruffed with dummy's Queen. If East overruffed his last two trumps would fall to South's Ace-Knave. So East did not ruff, but threw a Diamond.

Now came the critical trick. Declarer led me from dummy. If East ruffed, South would overruff, cash his highest trump, and East would make only one trump. Again, East played well—he declined to ruff, and again discarded a Diamond. On this trick South, as planned, discarded his remaining high Spade, so that his last four cards were all trumps. A Diamond was led from dummy and ruffed. That left South with the Ace-Knave-Six of trumps and East with the King-Ten-Eight. South led the Six, and however East plays, he can take only one trick. The doubled slam contract was made.

This I think, was an exceedingly well played hand. The declarer had to realise early on that, as he could not hope for a better Spade split than 5-2, his third high Spade was a liability and not an asset, and that to take its place a winner must be created in dummy that would keep the lead there and enable the embarrassing Spade to be got rid of at the right moment, if East refused to be lured into overruffing the Queen of trumps. Not many declarers would have analysed the hand so well as to discover soon enough in play the decisive importance I was going to assume in the end game.

* * *

"Good!" approved the King of Spades. "That is just the kind of thing I meant—something real and forthright."

He gave the gratified little Heart Six a rewarding pat on the head. This seemed to make another Six—the Six of Clubs—quite jealous.

"I don't deny the declarer played well," the Club Six said, captiously, "but after all he was handling plenty of good material. Indeed, he suffered from an embarrassment of riches, and his chief problem was to get rid of a superfluous winner. Now the hand I am going to tell Master Robert about, was one where the declarer had the absolute minimum for fulfilling his contract, if the opposing cards lay just right. With such skinny hands, it is generally the case that success is only possible if the play follows an exact order, from which any single deviation would be fatal. This hand, I think you will all agree, may be called—"

A LESSON IN TIMING

(*The Tale of the Six of Clubs*)

I HOLD NO BRIEF TO DEFEND THE BIDDING, BUT IT IS THE sort of thing that does happen at the bridge table with players who know they have the ability to get the last ounce out of their cards. These were the hands:

                    ♠ K Q 9 5 3 2
                    ♡ J 4 2
                    ◇ Q
                    ♣ 6 5 3

                         N
                    W   E
                         S

                    ♠ None
                    ♡ A K 10 3
                    ◇ A J 8 6 4 2
                    ♣ K 4 2

SOUTH	WEST	NORTH	EAST
1 ◇	No bid	1 ♠	1 N-T
3 ♡	No bid	4 ♡	No bid
6 ♡	No bid	No bid	Double
No bid	No bid	No bid	

West led the Four of Spades; dummy's Queen was covered by East's Ace; and South's Three of trumps took the trick. Although the declarer had politely said "Thank you, Partner" when dummy's cards went down, he was not very happy about the outcome. He felt rather like a stage manager with an incomplete cast. Trumps were short in both hands, and the opening lead had shortened South still more. There was only one trick in Spades. The Diamonds were far from being established. There were two or three possible losers in Clubs.

How to play the hand so as to take what chances there were of making the slam? The declarer soon gave up the idea of discarding dummy's Clubs on the Diamonds, and then ruffing a Club in dummy. The trumps would not hold out. The only alternative was to discard a Club on the established King of Spades. If the contract was to succeed, the Club King must be a trick. That is, the Ace must be with East, who had made a bid and doubled. Then the trumps must break 3-3, and the Queen must be with East. Finally, Diamonds, too, must break 3-3 or the King must be doubleton. It was asking rather much that the cards should lie just so, but when there is no other way to make a contract, a good player assumes everything lies right for him. In the same way it is the mark of the good player that when everything seems favourable for him, he looks around for unexpectedly bad distributions, and seeks means of guarding against them.

So the declarer cashed the Ace of Diamonds, and led a small Diamond, on which West dropped the King. The Deuce of trumps in dummy took the trick, and now the declarer led me. He did not relish having so soon to tackle the fragile Club suit, but it could not be postponed. East went up with the Ace, and returned a trump. South finessed the Ten, which held. As West was now void of Diamonds, the Knave of trumps in dummy had to be kept for the important duty of ruffing a Diamond, which was South's next lead. Then South's losing Club was discarded on the King of Spades, and the closed hand was entered with the King of Clubs. The Ace and King of Hearts drew the two remaining trumps in each of the opponent's hands, and South's remaining Diamonds were all tricks, East's Ten falling to the Knave.

The declarer's success was due not merely to the opposing cards lying favourably for him, but also to the correctness of the order in which he played the cards. The timing had to be perfect. As soon as the first Diamond is ruffed in dummy, a Club must be played at once. If dummy first plays the King of Spades for the Club discard, East will return a Spade when he gets in with the Ace of Clubs, and defeat the contract by shortening South's trumps. Similarly, it would be disastrous to draw a round of trumps after the first Diamond ruff. For after the second ruff the declarer would be faced by this losing dilemma: he either cashes the King of Spades before leading a Club from dummy, in which case East has the killing Spade return, or he must relinquish the Spade trick and lose two Clubs. The precise order in which the cards had to be played was here dictated by the very paucity of the material at the declarer's disposal.

* * *

Before the King of Spades could again express his approval, the philosophical Knave of Spades broke a silence which I felt had been unusually long for him to maintain.

"Hands like that one," he said, "seem to me to demonstrate admirably Bergson's distinction between time that is a reversible mathematical factor, with only an ideal existence, and time that is real irreversible duration. In bridge we do not talk of timing when the order of play is of little or no import, but only when the succession of tricks for the making or the breaking of a contract must be in a certain definite order admitting of no reversibility. Therefore timing at bridge has a reality of its own, and is no mere metaphor. I emphasise this because there are many players who think the terms 'timing' and 'tempo' are merely the grandiose invention of bridge writers, whereas they are but the expression of what becomes the very essence of play when there is conflict, when control is being fought for, when the contract is in danger."

This speech stunned the Little People for a few moments. Then the Five of Spades, with reluctant pride in his voice, said:

"Our Jack can go on for hours like that, if you let him. You see, Master Robert, he has a theory that bridge is a reflection of life—he calls it a microcosm, or something—and that all metaphysical beliefs find their counterparts there. But there's no doubt he is right about the hard reality of timing. That is strikingly illustrated in a hand in which I was the key card. But we've had one lesson on timing, so I'll call my story—"

A LESSON IN DETECTION

(The Tale of the Five of Spades)

♠ 4 3 2
♡ A Q 4
◇ 8 5 3
♣ 8 6 5 2

N
W   E
S

♠ A Q 6 5
♡ 7 5 2
◇ None
♣ A K Q J 10 9

Simple-looking hands, aren't they? The bidding, too, went simply, if rather over-optimistically by South. He began quietly with One Club. West passed, and North raised to Two Clubs. East passed, and South then jumped straight to Five Clubs, which all passed. I don't know why South imagined he could trust North, on his mere raise to Two Clubs, to be able to look after at least three of South's five and a half losers. I suppose South's void in Diamonds made him vaguely hope that North's raise was distributional and that he might get a cross-ruff going. If so, it must have been rather a shock to him to see North's completely balanced hand.

However, I didn't begin to look into South's mind closely until the first three tricks had been played. West led the King of Diamonds; East played the Queen to the trick; and South ruffed. Two rounds of trumps exhausted opponent's trumps, and South began to consider what next to do. He had even less material at his disposal for a high contract than did the declarer in the Club Six's tale.

As you all seem Sherlock Holmes fans, I should like at this stage to recall something that immortal detective said when he was investigating the disappearance of the famous race-horse, Silver Blaze, and the death of his trainer. Half-way through the investigation, Dr. Watson was in his usual state of bewilderment. To help him, Sherlock Holmes drew his attention to the significant behaviour during the night of the tragedy of the dog in the training stables. Watson pointed out that the dog had done nothing. That, Sherlock Holmes replied, was the significant behaviour.

Well, when I looked through South's eyes into his mind to see how he proposed to set about making eleven tricks I found he was doing exactly what Sherlock Holmes had done in drawing inferences from the dog's silence in the night. South was playing detective and drawing inferences from West's silence. I caught him arguing to himself.

"West led the King of Diamonds, and East played the Queen. That tells me West has the Ace of Diamonds. That is, he has two honour tricks. Also he was short in Clubs. Now if he had either the King of Spades or the King of Hearts, would he have said 'No bid' over my One Club? Of course not. And after North's mere raise to Two Clubs, would West have left my rather wild jump to Five Clubs undoubled, if he had held two and a half honour tricks? Not very likely. So I don't think I can look to West to hold either of the missing Kings.

♠ 4 3 2
♡ A Q 4
◇ 8 5 3
♣ 8 6 5 2

```
      N
  W       E
      S
```

♠ A Q 6 5
♡ 7 5 2
◇ None
♣ A K Q J 10 9

"If I'm right in that, the Heart finesse is hopeless, but the Spade finesse is O.K. Does that help me? I believe it does, for if the Spades break 3-3, I could afford to concede a Spade and then discard a losing Heart in dummy on the long Spade. But how am I going to lose a Spade safely? There's only one way.

And he made the strange play of leading me. West took the trick, and led a Heart. The declarer tried the finesse on the principle that you never can tell. As expected, East had the King, and returned a Heart. Dummy's Ace took the trick, and now a Spade was led, and the Queen successfully finessed. The Ace of Spades drew the remaining two Spades, and the Six of Spades became the thirteenth card, on which dummy's last Heart was discarded. Thus the contract was made, with the loss of only one Heart and one Spade.

South's success was due first to his detective ability in placing the two missing Kings and then his timing in the play of the Spade suit. As he had to lose a trick in the suit, he lost it at once, before he gave up control of Hearts. If he had led a Heart in order to get into dummy, the contract would have been defeated. If he had taken the Heart finesse, it would have failed, and the Heart return would have taken out the Ace. Then on getting in again with a Spade, the defence would have cashed a Heart trick. If

South had refrained from taking the Heart finesse, and entered dummy with the Ace, West, on taking the third round of Spades, would have led a Heart through the Queen to East's King-Knave, also breaking the contract. The vital question was when to lose the Spade trick that had to be lost, and the answer was "at once."

*　*　*

"I call that more a lesson in timing than in detection," remarked the King of Hearts. "Whatever his reasoning about the position of the Kings, the declarer must try both finesses, and he's all right as long as one of them comes off, provided he has first ducked a round of Spades."

"Yes, that is so," said the Knave of Diamonds; "but the Six of Clubs had got in before the Spade Five with the timing business, so what could the poor chap do but try to find what journalists term another angle? As a matter of fact, I am in the same position. The Spade Five in his turn has anticipated me, because the tale I have to tell is about detection and nothing but detection. Incidentally it is a hand in which Your Majesty was concerned"— and he bowed in the direction of the King of Hearts— "but, of course, I am the one most vitally implicated. My detective story hinges on a deduction from play, though the bidding, too, comes in; but it is based on the same principle as the Spade Five's tale. So I shall call it—"

THE DOG IN THE NIGHT AGAIN

(*The Tale of the Knave of Diamonds*)

CECIL BRAITHWAITE IS NO FAVOURITE OF MINE. I ADMIT HE'S harmless enough, but he's fat and conceited; and I don't like young men to be fat. Still less do I like fat young men when they boast of their bridge exploits—real or imagined. So I don't mind telling how he was taken down a peg or two. This feat was accomplished by Professor Hardacre in his quiet, amiable, lecturing way.

Our Cecil's overweening belief was in his ability to read opponent's hands. He was always saying things like—"At that stage I had a complete count on East's hand," "The declarer, of course, was marked with five Spades to the Ace-Queen and a singleton Club," "West's false-carding didn't help because by now I knew his cards to the last pip."

Well, there had been a stream of that sort of thing from him for about half an hour that evening in the cocktail bar before dinner, while Professor Hardacre sat over at a small table by the fire playing some complicated form of patience, apparently oblivious of what was going on around him. But not really so, for when Cecil's audience was showing signs of restiveness, the Professor suddenly broke up his patience and began to arrange the cards into two bridge hands. He called out to the group at the bar:

"You're a good card-reader, Braithwaite. At least, I've often heard you claim to be. Come and try your wits on this hand I had to play yesterday. It's rather a good one."

Cecil walked across to the Professor's table a little reluctantly, I thought, followed by his group of cronies.

"What tricky horror have you been cooking up now, Professor?" Cecil asked.

I said to myself: "Just so! He's getting ready what he and his crowd would incorrectly term an 'alibi' in case he falls down on the Professor's test."

But Professor Hardacre replied with unruffled amiability:

"No trick at all, my dear fellow. Just a hand that cropped up in a rubber yesterday, I assure you."

With suspicion still lurking in his eyes, Cecil looked at the cards the Professor had set out:

```
              ♠ Q 3
              ♡ A Q J
              ◇ 8 6 4
              ♣ A K Q J 5

                   N
            W           E
                   S

              ♠ K 10 5 2
              ♡ 10 9 8 6 5 2
              ◇ Q 3
              ♣ 4
```

The Professor gave the bidding, with both sides vulnerable, as:

East	South	West	North
1 ◇	No bid	No bid	Double
2 ◇	2 ♡	No bid	4 ♡
No bid	No bid	No bid	

"West led the Five of Diamonds," Professor Hardacre went on, "and East's King took the trick. East cashed the

183

♠ Q 3
♡ A Q J
♢ 8 6 4
♣ A K Q J 5

     N
W   E
     S

♠ K 10 5 2
♡ 10 9 8 6 5 2
♢ Q 3
♣ 4

Diamond Ace, West playing the Deuce. Then East laid down the Spade Ace, on which West played the Four. East next led the Six of Spades. Now you come in, Braithwaite. How do you play as declarer from this point?"

The fat young man pondered a few moments. Then he said:

"I don't see that there's much card-reading to be done here, Professor. And there's no need. The position is quite simple. To make the contract one must catch the King of Hearts. With nine cards, the proper thing is to finesse. The high cards already played by East fully justify his bidding, and therefore there's no reason why the Heart King should not be with West. However, I may have to finesse twice; so to minimise the risk of a Club overruff I take East's Spade lead with the King in the closed hand. Then I lead a Heart; finesse; and if it succeeds, I cash the Ace of Clubs, and return to South's hand with a Club ruff to take the second Heart finesse. Of course, if East has the King of Hearts or if all the Hearts are with West, the contract's sunk. I don't think there's much interest in this hand of yours, Professor. Wasn't that how you played it?"

"No, it wasn't," said Professor Hardacre, smiling broadly. "Really, Braithwaite, you disappoint me. I thought you prided yourself on card-reading, and you haven't even seen the opportunity for it on this hand. What I did was to take the Spade trick in South's hand just as you did, and lead a Heart. But I put up dummy's Ace, and dropped East's King."

"If you did that, Professor," exclaimed Cecil hotly, "it was just sheer luck. With nine cards, or even with ten, one must finesse against the King."

"No," returned the Professor, "it was not luck; it was card-reading. I drew what seems to me an obvious inference from East's play. But it was a negative inference. People draw positive inferences readily enough at bridge, but very few, it appears, look for negative inferences."

"What do you mean exactly by a negative inference, Professor?" asked one of the group.

"I mean drawing an inference from what a player has not done, instead of from what he has done."

Turning again to the puzzled Cecil, Professor Hardacre went on:

"Answer me this question: why didn't East lead the Knave of Diamonds after he had cashed the Ace of Spades, on which his partner had thrown a discouraging small card? Why did East not lead a third Diamond, when he and everyone else at the table knew West had no more Diamonds? Tell me that?"

"Well, that's not a hard one Professor," said Cecil after a moment's thought. "As East had the King of trumps himself, he knew West couldn't overruff, as it was pretty certain on the bidding that South had the Ten of trumps."

"Pretty certain, but not quite certain," the Professor pronounced. Then lecturing them gently, he continued: "The mere possession of the King of Hearts would not deter East from leading the Knave of Diamonds in the faint hope that West might have the Ten with which to overruff. That is surely a better lead than the useless Spade. But suppose East has the King of Hearts bare. Now he had a real motive for not leading a Diamond; now he is actually averse from letting the declarer know that West cannot overruff. If East had the King guarded, he wouldn't mind South knowing where the King lay; but with the singleton King, he would be careful not to reveal where it was. Hence his colourless Spade play. That is why I was quite confident that East had the bare King, and so was able to drop it by putting up the Ace."

For a moment Cecil tried to bluster it off.

"Really, you know, Professor," he began, "that's a bit far-fetched."

Then he observed how impressed the group was by Professor Hardacre's reasoning, and he gave in. And I'll say this for the fat young cub, he did it gracefully enough:

"You're dead right, Professor," he said. "Thanks for the tip. In future I'll add the 'negative inference' to my card-reading repertoire."

*   *   *

"I think you're rather hard on young Braithwaite," remonstrated the Ace of Spades. "He's quite a sound chap really. You must admit he's keen on the game, and if he's not as good an analyst as he thinks he is—well, he's in fairly wide company there, and anyway he has plenty of time to learn to justify his own opinion of himself."

Before the Knave of Diamonds could reply, the King of Hearts interposed querulously with:

"Oh, let the Diamond Knave air his prejudices. We all have 'em. But what I'm really annoyed at is his choosing a tale about my being a singleton. Damn it all, the deal I want to tell Master Robert of is also one in which I am alone—and in the East hand again. However, the point of my story is quite different. No clever card-reading or detection or timing."

"A good job too," called out the Eight of Clubs. "We've had enough 'lessons,' thank you."

"Actually, there are two points to my story," went on the Heart King. "The first point is that virtue is not automatically rewarded at bridge any more than it is in the world at large. Secondly, the hand is one more illustration—and I think a striking one—of the necessity to play for the improbable, if that's the only way to make or break a contract. It shows to what lengths a resourceful player will go when he is—"

UP AGAINST IT

(*The Tale of the King of Hearts*)

IT WAS A THIRD-ROUND MATCH FOR THE GOLD CUP, AND
the two teams were a contrast in methods. The one played
sound, steady orthodox Forcing-Two bridge. The other
four players were lively young sparks, who used a Two
Club system vigorously and believed in the forward game.

There were not many boards to go, and the orthodox team, after losing and regaining the lead several times, were now carefully cherishing an advantage of about a thousand points, while the other team were seeking opportunities for overtaking their rivals.

Then this deal came along, with both sides vulnerable:

```
                      ♠ Q 4
                      ♡ A J 9 5 3
                      ◇ 8 6 2
                      ♣ 8 6 3
         ♠ 7 6 5                    ♠ K 9 3
         ♡ 10 8 6 4 2    N          ♡ K
         ◇ K Q 10      W   E        ◇ 9 7 5 4
         ♣ 5 2            S         ♣ J 10 9 7 4
                      ♠ A J 10 8 2
                      ♡ Q 7
                      ◇ A J 3
                      ♣ A K Q
```

At the table where orthodoxy held the North-South cards, the bidding went:

South	North
1 ♠	2 ♡
3 ♠	4 ♠
No bid	

West led the King of Diamonds, and South ducked, preparing a Bath Coup for West if he continued the suit.

190

But West switched to the Four of Hearts. The declarer finessed, and I made the trick for East, who promptly returned a Diamond. South's Ace won; and, wishing to get into dummy, he led his Queen of Hearts, and overtook with dummy's Ace. East ruffed, and returned another Diamond. West's Queen made, and West led a Club. Declarer now had to lose another trick to the King of Spades. So he was two down, the defence making two Diamonds, a Heart, a Heart ruff, and a trump trick—a penalty of 200 points.

The players analysed the hand, and agreed that South had played correctly. He had been defeated only by unfavourable distribution of suits and opposing high cards.

In the other room, where youth and vigour, eager for slams, sat North-South, the bidding was very different. I had better mention that they were using the Culbertson Four-Five No-Trumps convention.

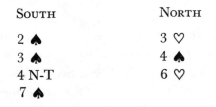

SOUTH	NORTH
2 ♠	3 ♡
3 ♠	4 ♠
4 N-T	6 ♡
7 ♠	

Again the opening lead was the King of Diamonds, South's Ace taking the trick. Grand Slams don't admit of Bath Coups! South now led the Queen of Hearts, and West played low. The declarer paused to consider. He needed two entries to the table—one to take the trump

```
              ♠ Q 4
              ♡ A J 9 5 3
              ♢ 8 6 2
              ♣ 8 6 3
♠ 7 6 5                        ♠ K 9 3
♡ 10 8 6 4 2      N            ♡ K
♢ K Q 10     W       E         ♢ 9 7 5 4
♣ 5 2             S            ♣ J 10 9 7 4
              ♠ A J 10 8 2
              ♡ Q 7
              ♢ A J 3
              ♣ A K Q
```

finesse and the other for access to the Hearts. He realised, as he put it to himself, that he was "up against it." If West had the King, the contract was impossible for lack of the second entry. It was equally impossible if East had the King guarded. Therefore the one and only hope was that East held the singleton King, improbable as that was. Then dummy would have two entries—the Heart Ace and the Heart Knave-Nine over West's Ten-Eight. So, with a shrug, the declarer overtook his Queen with dummy's Ace, and I dropped to the trick. Now the Queen of Spades was led, and the King caught.

The declarer then played out all his Spades and Clubs, and West was squeezed in Hearts and Diamonds for the Grand Slam to be made scoring 2,210.

The result was this monstrous piece of injustice: a contract of Four Spades was defeated by two tricks, despite faultless dummy play, while Seven Spades was made with the same cards by a player who declined to finesse against the King with six of the suit in the opposing hands—a swing of 2,410 points.

*   *   *

It was too much to expect the philosopher of the Pack to let this story pass without comment.

"One more illustration," claimed the Knave of Spades,

"of my contention that bridge is a miniature mirror of life. In bridge and in life alike you search in vain for justice. Opportunists snatch the sweets from under the noses of the sound and steady. Luck falls with the haphazardness of bombs in an air raid. In life the careful man has his savings taken from him by inflation, while the spendthrift somehow finds enough in his pocket for the day's pleasure; and in bridge the faultless bidder, playing impeccably, is defeated by improbable distribution which the declarer who has blundered into a fantastic contract is forced by the inventiveness of desperation to turn to his own account. In bridge and in life I fear it is the truth that virtue has indeed to be its own reward."

"Stuff and nonsense!" exclaimed the Ten of Diamonds. "I don't know much about life, and I don't believe the Spade Knave does either. After all, we only know of it through what we see of humans when they handle us and the little we can read in their minds. But in bridge I affirm that there is justice. The injustice we see at the card table is short-term injustice. In the long run the best players win; in the long run obedience to mathematical probabilities pays; in the long run the sound and steady beat the erratically brilliant just as certainly and inevitably as they do the mediocre, who may go off with a packet at the end of any particular session if Brigidda feels that way and showers all the high cards on them."

"By and large that's true enough, Ten," put in the Three of Diamonds. "But I know of a case of what you'd call short-term injustice—for it centred on one deal—which lasted a lifetime. I was reminded of it by the Heart King's remark that you can't prepare a Bath Coup in a Grand Slam hand. His Majesty told of good play that lost a match. I tell of superb play that penalised a player for the rest of his days. However, though the injustice is clamant, there is, perhaps, little cause for tears, as you may guess when I say that my choice of title is—"

MILLIONAIRE FAUTE DE MIEUX

(*The Tale of the Three of Diamonds*)

YOU'VE NO DOUBT HEARD, MASTER ROBERT, OF LORD Halogen, the shipping magnate. Well, if you should ever chance to be a guest of his—and he is very hospitable—you will find hanging in isolation on one wall of his study in his sumptuous country house a strange thing. It is a large black picture frame, with an expanse of white mount, in the centre of which is a playing card. That card is I—the Three of Diamonds.

If he takes you off to his study after dinner for a chat, as is his custom with favoured guests, you will wonder at my so elaborate presence among the priceless masterpieces that look down on you from the other walls of the room. Lord Halogen will notice your surprise, and smile.

"A reminder," he will say, "of what might have been. A memorial to a departed reputation. Also the beginning of me as a person of weight in affairs which the world thinks are of importance. Perhaps you would care to hear about it?"

And of course you will say you would. Then, with the two of you smoking big fat cigars and sipping from elegant glasses at your elbows, he will take a pack of cards from the drawer of his desk, spread out a bridge deal before you, and tell you this tale. I have heard him tell it countless times, and always with the same touch of bitter, regretful humour. I can vouch, since I was so vitally involved, for the deal and the bidding and play; but for the sequel— well, Lord Halogen is not the man to let a story lose in the telling. However, you shall judge for yourselves.

"When I was a young man," he will say, "and supposed to be making my way in the shipping firm into which my father had got me by making use of the fact that he and the senior partner had been bosom friends at school, I developed for bridge a passion that merited the epithet of grand. I gave the game all my spare time and some of which I robbed my employers. While I carefully studied bidding, it was the play of the cards that enthralled me beyond words. And, inevitably, I dreamed of becoming a master player, of being asked to join a first-rate team, and of winning national contests and, eventually, international fame.

"I had advanced some little way along this ambitious path. I was acquiring a reputation as a sound bidder and a skilful player, and was beginning to be sought after by team captains for minor events. Then, one day, when I was playing in a well-known club, where reputations are hard to gain and easy to mar, I dealt these cards sitting South:

```
                ♠ K 4 2
                ♡ 5 4 3
                ◇ A 10 3
                ♣ A 8 6 2
   ♠ Q 10 7 6       N        ♠ J 9 8 5
   ♡ 9 7                     ♡ Q J 10 8 2
   ◇ K Q J 5 4  W     E      ◇ 9 8 6
   ♣ 5 3           S         ♣ 4
                ♠ A 3
                ♡ A K 6
                ◇ 7 2
                ♣ K Q J 10 9 7
```

"We were vulnerable, and they were not, and the bidding went:

South	West	North	East
1 ♣	1 ◇	2 N-T	3 ♡
Double	No bid	4 ♣	No bid
4 N-T	No bid	5 N-T	No bid
6 ♣	No bid	7 ♣	No bid
No bid	Double	No bid	No bid
No bid			

197

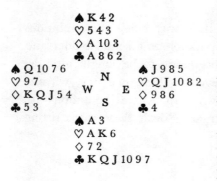

```
              ♠ K 4 2
              ♡ 5 4 3
              ◇ A 10 3
              ♣ A 8 6 2
♠ Q 10 7 6              ♠ J 9 8 5
♡ 9 7         N         ♡ Q J 10 8 2
◇ K Q J 5 4 W   E       ◇ 9 8 6
♣ 5 3         S         ♣ 4
              ♠ A 3
              ♡ A K 6
              ◇ 7 2
              ♣ K Q J 10 9 7
```

"West led the King of Diamonds, and North tabled his hand. I saw at once that he had grossly overbid his cards, and that between us we had only eleven winners. I examined the chances of developing the two extra tricks. It would have to be done by a triple progressive squeeze. Did the requirements for that exist? Only if all the three side suits were held in one of the opponents' hands, with no stopper to any of them in the other hand. Clearly, as West had led the King of Diamonds, it was only possible to imagine that situation existing in West's hand. Could that be, even if I ignored the bidding? Any three Spades in East's hand would constitute a stopper. Therefore West must hold six Spades. Similarly he must have five Hearts and three Diamonds. But that counted to fourteen cards.

"Obviously, then, the Grand Slam could not be there—unless opponents made mistakes. Should I hope for that, and stage a pseudo-squeeze? But my opponents were good players, and even if they did slip up, I could not see that one or two bad discards would help me. So I gave up all idea of making the Grand Slam, and to this day I think that decision was right.

"The question then arose: Could I make twelve tricks, and reduce a 500 penalty to 200? I now took the bidding into account—Diamonds bid by West and Hearts by East, and concluded that a true double squeeze, with both opponents being squeezed at the same trick, was possible as both of them would be obliged to protect Spades. But to rectify the count and make the squeeze position possible, I must first lose a trick. Which trick? To lose a trick in Spades or Hearts would be bad, as in either case I should be giving up a card needed for the squeeze. So it had to be a Diamond trick. But clearly I dared not take the first trick with dummy's Ace and return a Diamond, as West would lead back a third Diamond. I could ruff this, of course, but then I would have no Diamond left for the end-play.

"So was it that I decided to duck the opening lead, and instead of putting on dummy's Ace, I played dummy's Three of Diamonds.

"As I threw that Three of Diamonds on the trick, I little thought it was to prove my complete undoing. My partner's eyebrows shot up indignantly. My two opponents sniggered.

" 'Wait,' I thought to myself, 'you'll soon see how well I'm playing this hand.'

"West continued with the Queen of Diamonds. This trick I took with dummy's Ace. I then cashed the Ace of Spades, the Ace and King of Heart and five trumps, leaving the remaining cards distributed like this:

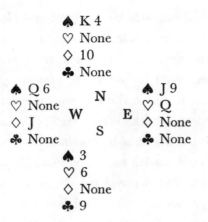

```
              ♠ K 4
              ♡ None
              ◇ 10
              ♣ None
   ♠ Q 6          N          ♠ J 9
   ♡ None                    ♡ Q
   ◇ J        W      E       ◇ None
   ♣ None         S          ♣ None
              ♠ 3
              ♡ 6
              ◇ None
              ♣ 9
```

"I now led my squeeze card, the Nine of Clubs. West had to keep the Diamond Knave, and so threw his Six of Spades. I discarded dummy's Diamond Ten. Now East was in trouble. Hoping his partner had the thirteenth Heart, he threw the Queen, not daring to unguard the Knave of Spades. So I made the last two tricks with the Six of Hearts and the King of Spades. But however they had discarded, they were helpless. It was a perfect classical double squeeze.

"Did I get any recognition for this fine performance—as I still contend it was—from my partner or opponents? I did not. All my partner would say was that it was unheard of to duck to the first trick in a Grand Slam contract, and that I should have gone up with the Ace and hoped for opponents to make mistakes in defence. All my opponents would do was to laugh. I was so indignant that, in my folly, I would not let the matter rest there. I appealed to everybody I met to say whether I had acted rightly or not. None of them listened beyond the first trick. As soon as I said I had ducked the opening lead, they waved a hand at me in derision, and walked away.

"And so the play of that innocent-looking Three of Diamonds ruined my bridge career. I simply became known as the man who had ducked to the first trick in a Grand Slam. No more captains wanted me in their teams. People fought shy of playing with me at partnership sessions. As a bridge player, I was a man with a bee in his bonnet who was, to boot, a defeatist in play.

"Eventually I saw it was hopeless, and I turned my attention to my job in the shipping office. I shunned bridge clubs, and gave all my energies to the coming and going of ships and their cargoes. I found they, too, had their fascination, and so in time I became what to-day you see I am—a person who matters in the world of commerce. But I might have been, I still maintain, a great bridge player. Anyway, I like to think so. And I keep that Three of Diamonds there on my wall to remind myself that it is always possible to be too good; that ideal excellence is not enough—it's a damn sight too much; and that in every walk of life there are some things that are simply not done, even if they ought to be. I have profited in my commercial career by remembering the lesson that, in bridge, one of those things is to decline to take the first trick in a Grand Slam contract."

* * *

This story affected the Wee Folk variously. Some sided with Lord Halogen, and praised his cool realism in deciding against a quixotic attempt on the impossible; others took the line that, however hopeless the contract might seem, no player should abandon its fulfilment right at the outset. Then the Knave of Clubs spoke.

"I don't care a fig for the rights or wrongs of the matter," he declared. "What pleases me is the exquisite captivation of that double squeeze, which turned the third card of an Ace-King-Six suit into a winner. I like to count myself a humble camp-follower of those great analysts who find a peculiar charm in squeezes. The mysterious way they work, producing something out of nothing or next door to nothing. For what sort of an asset is the third card of an Ace-King-Six suit? The cunning way they entail so often the surrender of one or two tricks in apparent generosity. The ruthless way they make seemingly certain tricks in opponents' hands melt away. No matter how long you study the mechanics of squeezes, you'll never be disillusioned; nothing can cause them to lose their affinity to sheer witchcraft."

"How true, how true!" said the Seven of Hearts lyrically. "The smooth inexorability of your true squeeze has the terrible beauty of Fate—The pity is that squeezes are almost always the perquisite of declarers. Defenders are so seldom able to use the device, partly because it is hard for them to read the situation of the cards in time, and partly because of the added difficulty of partnership co-operation. But sometimes it happens that one defender alone can control the play, and then he may be able to bring off a squeeze. One of my happiest memories is just such an occasion. It was no simple type of squeeze, either; and it was distinguished by a feature which I think might be picturesquely described as—"

A TROJAN HORSE

(*The Tale of the Seven of Hearts*)

SO RARE IS IT FOR A DEFENDER TO EXECUTE A SQUEEZE
that when it does happen, the declarer is almost always
taken by surprise. It was so in this case, in which I was dealt
to East among as ordinary a collection of cards as you could
imagine:

```
              ♠ J 10 3
              ♡ K J 10 8
              ◇ 9 6 5 4 2
              ♣ 6
♠ 8 4                           ♠ Q 7 6 5
♡ 9 3            N              ♡ A 7 5 2
◇ 8 7      W         E          ◇ A K 10
♣ A 10 9 8 7 5 2    S           ♣ 4 3
              ♠ A K 9 2
              ♡ Q 6 4
              ◇ Q J 3
              ♣ K Q J
```

North-South had a part-score of 30 in the third game of the rubber, and East was dealer. The part-score situation may excuse, even though it may not justify, the bidding, which went:

EAST	SOUTH	WEST	NORTH
1 N-T	Double	2 ♣	2 ◇
No bid	2 N-T	No bid	No bid
No bid			

West led off with the Ten of Clubs, which South's King took. The declarer cashed his King of Spades, on which he played dummy's Three, and then led the Queen of Hearts. East played low to the trick, and when another Heart was led, also allowed dummy's Ten to win. Dummy's Knave of Spades was led and run, East playing low. The Spade Ten was led, and again East declined to cover. The declarer had won six tricks—three Spades, two Hearts,

and a Club. A Diamond was led from dummy. East took
the trick with his King, and cashed his Ace of Hearts. The
situation now was:

```
                    ♠ None
                    ♡ J
                    ◇ 9 6 5 4
                    ♣ None
  ♠ None                        ♠ Q
  ♡ None          N             ♡ 7
  ◇ None      W       E         ◇ A 10
  ♣ A 9 8 7 5     S             ♣ 4
                    ♠ A
                    ♡ None
                    ◇ Q J
                    ♣ Q J
```

East paused to consider what best to do. There was little
doubt that the declarer's last five cards were the Ace of
Spades, two Diamonds and two Clubs. If he had the Ace
of Clubs, he must make his contract. But if West had the
Ace, there was still hope of doing something. East asked
himself whether he should lead a Club at once. He decided
against that, for, if South held the Queen-Knave, as seemed
likely from West's lead of the Ten, to do so would set up
a trick for South. So would the play of the Ace of Diamonds,
and the lead of the Spade was obviously bad. So that left
only—

East found himself staring at me. He saw it then, and,
with a smile of anticipation, led me.

The declarer's face brightened when he found me on

the green cloth in front of him. He began to chaff East.

"So that's what you play after that long trance," he said. "Why, my dear fellow, if you could only count to thirteen you would know that I have no Heart, and could never have got dummy to cash the Knave without your kindly help. It's a real gift."

"*Timeo Danaos et dona ferentes.* You remember your Virgil?" said East.

But South, who didn't, replied: "Let's get on with the game," and looked at his hand to decide what to play from it to the trick.

Nothing was further from his thoughts than that I was a squeeze-card; but his brow began to darken as he slowly realised he had no satisfactory discard. Finally he let go the Ace of Spades, remarking, with rather forced cheerfulness:

"Well, exchange is no robbery. If I don't make the Ace of Spades, I'm making the Knave of Hearts."

Dummy had nothing but Diamonds to lead. East made his Diamond Ace, and played the Queen of Spades. Then, at last, South realised that the outrageous was happening— he, the declarer, was being deliberately squeezed. He threw the Knave of Clubs, and now East led that suit, enabling West to take the last two tricks and defeat the contract.

"Well, I'm damned!" exclaimed South in an injured voice. "That was a perfect progressive squeeze, set going by your giving me a trick I couldn't otherwise make, but gaining for you two tricks in its place. I've never seen such a thing done by the defence against a declarer."

"I told you the Seven of Hearts was a Greek gift," said East. "It was a wooden horse."

South, who had been on the Modern Side at school, merely repeated;

"Well, I'm damned!"

* * *

I was astonished at the enthusiastic applause that broke out as the Heart Seven ceased. Plainly, the People of the Pack were keen connoisseurs of squeezes.

"A veritable museum piece," pronounced the King of Diamonds.

"In defensive play that hand makes history," was the appraisement of the Ace of Clubs.

"It was indeed a highly unusual exploit," remarked the Knave of Spades in his precise way. "But East went somewhat astray as a classical scholar in describing the play of the Heart Seven as a Greek gift. The Trojans need not have allowed the wooden horse inside their city, but the declarer had no choice. The essence of a Greek gift is that it can be refused. I think the lead of the Heart Seven can more flatly be compared to the poisoned wine of the Borgias. The wretched victims of that magnificent family were seldom in a position to decline the courteously offered draught."

"Our Jack's at it again," exclaimed the Four of Spades. "There never was such a pedantic fellow. But whether the Heart Seven was a Greek gift or a lethal potion, I am going to cap his story. A progressive squeeze in defence is a rarity, I admit, but have you ever heard, Master Robert, of a defensive Grand Coup? That is a feat I performed at the command of the player who held me. He knew the game, I can tell you! I shall never forget how promptly he realised that the one and only way to break the contract was for him to become—"

A PRODIGAL IN TRUMPS

(*The Tale of the Four of Spades*)

I FOUND MYSELF IN THE WEST HAND WITH FOUR MORE OF
my tribe to the Knave, and was therefore rather surprised
to hear South open the bidding with One Spade, and still
more surprised when North jumped straight to Four Spades.

My man led the Queen of Clubs, and when dummy went down, these were the twenty-six cards West could see:

```
                  ♠ 7 6 5 3
                  ♡ 10 8 7 6 5 4
                  ◇ A 4
                  ♣ 3
   ♠ J 9 8 4 2          N
   ♡ 3
   ◇ Q 8 6         W          E
   ♣ Q J 10 8           S
```

The Queen of Clubs turned out to be rather an unlucky lead. South took the trick with the Ace in his own hand, and ruffed a Club in dummy. He returned to the closed hand with the Ace of Hearts, and ruffed another Club. Then he led a trump from dummy. East showed out, discarding the Knave of Diamonds, and South took the trick with the Ace of trumps. For the third time he ruffed a Club in dummy, East dropping the Club King. A Heart was now led from dummy. East put on the Knave and South the Deuce.

Before playing to the trick, my man, West, considered the situation, and counted South's hand. He had three trumps, the King-Queen-Ten. He had just played the Deuce of Hearts, and his other three cards must be Diamonds— three small Diamonds according to East's signal with the Knave of Diamonds. Therefore, the situation at the second Heart lead must be:

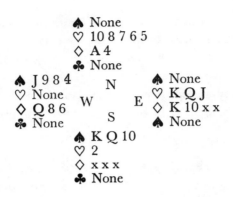

♠ None
♡ 10 8 7 6 5
◇ A 4
♣ None

♠ J 9 8 4   N   ♠ None
♡ None   ♡ K Q J
◇ Q 8 6 W   E ◇ K 10 x x
♣ None   S   ♣ None

♠ K Q 10
♡ 2
◇ x x x
♣ None

Declarer already had six tricks. If he could make the Ace of Diamonds and his three remaining trumps, he had his contract. Nothing could stop him from making the Ace of Diamonds or the King-Queen of trumps. Therefore the one chance left the defence was to prevent the Ten of trumps from becoming a trick. My man's Knave must kill it. For that to happen, clearly West had a superfluity of trumps. He must embark on trump reducing play to bring the number of his trumps down to parity with South's trumps.

West hesitated no longer. He ruffed his partner's master Knave of Hearts with me—the Grand Coup in defence!

West rid himself of the lead by playing the Queen of Diamonds, dummy's Ace took, and a Heart was led, South ruffing with the King. A new wile, this, by the declarer; but my man was equal to it. He under-ruffed with the Eight of Spades, thereby still keeping trump parity with South. That individual now tried to throw the lead to West with a Diamond, but East took the trick, and his return of a Heart finally broke the contract. For if South does not ruff, West still has a Diamond to throw on the trick, leaving the lead with East to play through South's Queen-Ten of trumps to West's Knave-Nine. A perfect Trump Coup in defence, in the preparation of which the Grand Coup—the ruffing of a winning card in order to shorten trumps—was executed.

* * *

Again a salvo of applause greeted the end of the tale, and the Queen of Hearts seemed to sum up the general feeling when she remarked contentedly:

"It's nice to hear of defenders coming into their own. We've been having such a lot of stories about clever declarers."

"Talking of cleverness," said the Ace of Diamonds, "I've often wondered why the Grand Coup is given such a magniloquent name. Once a player has made up his mind that his proper course is to reduce the number of his trumps, there's nothing particularly clever in taking the opportunity to shed a trump by ruffing a winner. There are many far more difficult coups than that with less high-sounding titles, while some are even nameless."

"Yes," interposed the Knave of Hearts, "the very hand I want to tell Master Robert about was the occasion for a most skilful type of defence with no exalted name. It, too, was concerned with trump embarrassment, but for quite a different reason. It called for great foresight to see the threatened danger in time to dodge it. And dodging it involved something that must always be particularly distasteful to a defender—nothing less than—"

THROWING AWAY A TRUMP TRICK

(*The Tale of the Knave of Hearts*)

WHEN I WAS DEALT TO WEST, AND FOUND THAT I AND THE Knave of Clubs were his two highest cards, I little thought the whole of the play was to turn on the way I was handled. With North-South only vulnerable, the adventure began with some exciting bidding.

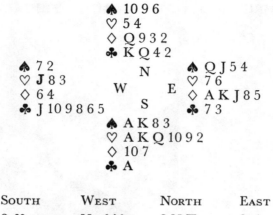

♠ 10 9 6
♡ 5 4
◇ Q 9 3 2
♣ K Q 4 2

♠ 7 2
♡ **J** 8 3
◇ 6 4
♣ J 10 9 8 6 5

W   N   E
S

♠ Q J 5 4
♡ 7 6
◇ A K J 8 5
♣ 7 3

♠ A K 8 3
♡ A K Q 10 9 2
◇ 10 7
♣ A

SOUTH	WEST	NORTH	EAST
2 ♡	No bid	2 N-T	3 ◇
No bid	No bid	Double	3 ♠
Double	4 ♣	Double	No bid
4 ♡	No bid	No bid	No bid

West led the Six of Diamonds; dummy played low; and East took the trick with his Knave. He cashed the King of Diamonds, and then led the Five of the suit. Whereupon the declarer went into a bit of a huddle; and when East saw that, he began to smile and to preen himself on having put his opponent into a hole by setting up a trump trick in West's hand, for what else could South be worrying about but an overruff?

Meanwhile, I became aware that my man, West, was thinking hard, too. Why? I gazed deep into his eyes, and perceived that he was saying:

"My partner bid Diamonds, and had Ace-King-Knave. Then he bid Spades, and that can't be a psych either; so he must have something in Spades. And South declined to leave the double of Clubs in. Clearly South is very short in Clubs. I bet he has a void or singleton—probably the Ace. In either case, he has no possible hope of getting into dummy to cash the Clubs, unless—. Yes, I see my danger now."

At this moment the declarer came to a decision, and ruffed the trick with the Queen. Without hesitation, West seized me, and played me to the trick. East glared angrily across at West. South looked surprised, but not at all pleased. He knew only too well that his one chance of making his contract had vanished. Do what he could, he could not enter dummy, and had to lose two Spade tricks to East.

"You see now how it was," said my man to East, whose momentary annoyance had gone. "I had to take advantage of your sound lead of the Diamond to get out from under. If I don't exit with the Knave of trumps, South strips my hand by cashing Ace-King of Spades, and the Ace of Clubs. Then he throws me in with a trump, and I should have to lead a Club to dummy. It was lucky I sized up the situation in time."

*   *   *

The Knave of Clubs seemed the only one who wanted to comment. "I'll bet West enjoyed himself in that hand," he remarked gloatingly. "There can be nothing more satisfactory to a defender than to take some action early that he knows makes the eventual defeat of the contract a certainty, and then sit back and watch the declarer wriggle. And" he added, hastily—"I don't need the Spade Knave to tell me that's simply sadism. To which my answer is 'So what?' For I agree with him that at the bridge table, as in life, people have mixed motives and seek satisfaction for all sorts

215

of hidden cravings. The only difference is that at bridge it is all quite harmless, as long as the outward courtesies are maintained. You may impale your opponent and take pleasure in his subsequent agonies, provided you don't let him see your delight."

"There's much too much philosophising at this party," the Ace of Spades interrupted brusquely. "We're here to entertain Master Robert, not try to impress him with our learning and culture, as some of us seem to think. What he wants to hear about, I'm sure, is the most interesting or exciting hand each of us has figured in. Now, curiously enough, my most thrilling memory is not of actual play, but of a post-mortem. Plenty of emotion, as in most post-mortems, and even, for ought I can tell, sadism involved. But at bottom a problem simply of best defence against best attack. Which is bridge at its highest level. And for reasons that will transpire, I shall call it—"

A FEAT OF ILLUSION

(*The Tale of the Ace of Spades*)

OFERINI WAS NIGHTLY MYSTIFYING A PACKED COLISEUM
with the appearances and disappearances that had made
him world-famous as a magician. Some nights, when the
show was over and his audiences were on their way home
telling each other, unconvinced and unconvincingly, that
it was "all done with mirrors," the great illusionist would
stroll into this club for a rubber or two. Once, when it was

later than he had realised, he found the bridge-room deserted save for a small knot of people round one table, where two erstwhile players were arguing strenuously over a deal spread out before them. This was it:

♠ None
♡ A 10 8 3
♦ Q 4 3 2
♣ A K 7 5 2

♠ A 10 8 6 5 3
♡ Q J 9 6 4
♦ 8
♣ 8

♠ 7 2
♡ 7 5
♦ K J 10 7
♣ Q J 10 9 4

♠ K Q J 9 4
♡ K 2
♦ A 9 6 5
♣ 6 3

Both men were fairly good players, but, like so many fairly good players, they thought themselves much better than that. Temperamentally they were in contrast. One was all ebullience; the other affected a cool disdain of any view that differed from his. So, as their real names don't matter, let us call them Mr. Hot and Mr. Cold.

They had been partners with the North-South hands, had contracted to make Three No-Trumps, and had been two tricks down. Now they were criticising each other's bidding; and when Oferini joined the group of spectators, they had agreed that a Diamond contract was best, and had reached the stage of disputing about the number of tricks South could make in that denomination.

Cold: "Well, I would undertake to make at least Three

Diamonds, with one Spade ruff, one Spade trick, two Heart tricks, two Club ruffs, two Club tricks, and the Ace of trumps."

Hot: "Who ever heard of counting to and fro ruffs in that crazy fashion? But if you are going to analyse the hand that way, you might as well be accurate. South can make more tricks than you can count on your fingers."

Cold: "You exaggerate. I said nine tricks at least, but I believe South could make ten tricks. That, however, is the limit."

Hot: "Is it, indeed? But let us first hear how you propose to make your ten tricks."

Cold: "What is West's opening lead?"

Hot: "In this hand that's unimportant. We'll say the Eight of Clubs."

Cold: "In that case I win with the Ace, and cash the Ace of Diamonds to strip West of his single trump. Next I lead a high Spade. West covers with the Ace, and dummy ruffs. I cash the King of Clubs, and ruff a Club. Returning to the table with the Ace of Hearts, I ruff another Club. I cash the King of Hearts and a high Spade. Then I lead a small Spade. West covers, and I let him hold the trick; I don't ruff in dummy. West returns another Spade, and again I don't ruff in dummy. But East has nothing but trumps left; is forced to ruff; and now has to lead a trump, so that the Queen of Diamonds in dummy must make, giving me my tenth trick. So I make just Four Diamonds."

The kibitzers murmured admiring agreement.

Hot: "What livid nonsense! I tell you I can make one

```
            ♠ None
            ♡ A 10 8 3
            ◇ Q 4 3 2
            ♣ A K 7 5 2
♠ A 10 8 6 5 3          ♠ 7 2
♡ Q J 9 6 4      N      ♡ 7 5
◇ 8          W     E    ◇ K J 10 7
♣ 8              S      ♣ Q J 10 9 4
            ♠ K Q J 9 4
            ♡ K 2
            ◇ A 9 6 5
            ♣ 6 3
```

more trick than you—as I usually do. I can make game in Diamonds."

Cold: "I double your Five Diamonds."

Hot: "I redouble. And for ten pounds, if you dare take the bet."

Cold: "Done! I'll give you the same lead of the Eight of Clubs."

Hot: "Here goes. First trick, Ace of Clubs. Second, Ace of Diamonds. Third, King of Clubs. Fourth, Club ruff. Fifth, a Spade honour, covered and ruffed. Sixth, Club ruff. Seventh, Ace of Hearts. Eighth, Club ruff. Ninth, King of Hearts. Tenth, a high Spade. Eleventh, another high Spade, on which dummy discards his last Heart. East has now only three trumps. He must take the trick and play away from his tenace. Superficially I have taken the same line as you, but I have managed to make one trick more."

At this there was much excitement amongst the kibitzers. Cold took out his wallet, and handed Hot two five-pound notes. It was at this moment that Oferini stepped out of the group of spectators. Smiling pleasantly at Mr. Hot, he asked:

"Would you care to bet me you can make Five Diamonds a second time?"

Hot mockingly replied:

"My dear Oferini, have you so much superfluous money?"

"Yes. I have just ten pounds more than I need."

"Go ahead, then. You conduct the defence."

"Well, Hot, I'm a generous fellow," remarked Oferini; "and so I'll lead off with the Ace of Spades and set up three Spade tricks for you."

For several minutes Hot wrestled with the new problem, and then admitted himself beaten. Oferini's lead had robbed dummy of an entry, and it was no longer possible to ruff all dummy's small Clubs.

"I had overlooked this variation in the defence," said Hot. "Only ten tricks can be made. Cold is right after all."

"No, I'm not," interposed Cold, as Hot handed the ten pounds over to Oferini. "I will show you, if you will give me a chance to win back my stake, that I can sometimes make a trick more than you."

"Right you are," said Hot. "Although Oferini has robbed me of what you paid me, I'll gladly give you a tenner if you can make eleven tricks against that lead of the Ace of Spades."

"This is how to play it," said Cold. "I ruff the Spade Ace, and lead the Deuce of trumps. East puts on the Ten, and South's Ace wins. He cashes a Spade honour, dummy discarding a Club. The Heart King and Ace are cashed, and now dummy leads a Heart. What do you play as East, Hot?"

The position then was:

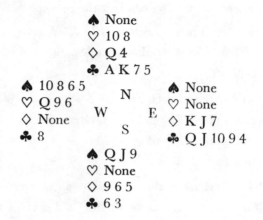

```
                    ♠ None
                    ♡ 10 8
                    ◇ Q 4
                    ♣ A K 7 5
  ♠ 10 8 6 5          N          ♠ None
  ♡ Q 9 6                         ♡ None
  ◇ None        W         E       ◇ K J 7
  ♣ 8                S            ♣ Q J 10 9 4
                    ♠ Q J 9
                    ♡ None
                    ◇ 9 6 5
                    ♣ 6 3
```

Hot analysed aloud:

"If I discard a Club, South ruffs and plays over to the
Ace of Clubs. Another Heart is led. Unless I ruff high,
South ruffs again; enters dummy with the King of Clubs,
and ruffs a Club. Now I'm again down to three trumps
and must ruff South's Spade lead, while the table discards
its last Club. The Queen of trumps must then make. Oh,
darn the thing. That means I must ruff one of the Hearts.
The first? No! South would discard his small Spade on my
Diamond Knave, and I would make only the two trump
honours."

Cold: "I'm waiting for your decision. That is all that
interests me."

Hot: "Damnation! I discard a Club."

Cold: "I ruff; cross to dummy with the Ace of Clubs;
and lead a Heart. Your play!"

♠ None
♥ 10 8
♦ Q 4
♣ A K 7 5

♠ 10 8 6 5   **N**   ♠ None
♥ Q 9 6 **W**   **E** ♥ None
♦ None   **S**   ♦ K J 7
♣ 8   ♣ Q J 10 9 4

♠ Q J 9
♥ None
♦ 9 6 5
♣ 6 3

"Hot: "I ruff with the Knave; cash the Diamond King; and teach you not to boast by throwing the lead to dummy with my last trump, and the table must play Clubs to me."

Cold: "Just a moment. Dummy's Queen of trumps is thrown on your lead of the King, and I make eleven tricks."

Hot stared at the cards in silence, and then took out two more five-pound notes, and handed them to Cold, who thanked him politely, and turned to Oferini.

"Can you, perhaps, beat my play?"

"I think I can. Do you care to bet?"

"Indeed, yes. There's ten pounds waiting for you if you can do it. Shall we take the play up from where dummy leads a Heart after the Ace and King have been cashed?"

"Agreed. I discard a Club."

"I ruff," purred Cold, "and after crossing to dummy with the Ace of Clubs, I lead another Heart."

"I ruff with the Knave," said Oferini, "and lead the Queen of Clubs."

Cold stared aghast at the cards. The whole situation was altered. Nothing he could do could now prevent East from making a trick with his Seven of trumps.

Hot's good humour returned. He exclaimed:

"What a chap you are Oferini! You separate me from Cold's money, and Cold from my money. Good luck to you!"

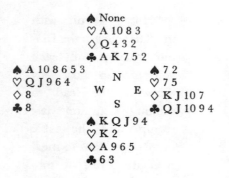

♠ None
♡ A 10 8 3
◊ Q 4 3 2
♣ A K 7 5 2

♠ A 10 8 6 5 3
♡ Q J 9 6 4
◊ 8
♣ 8

♠ 7 2
♡ 7 5
◊ K J 10 7
♣ Q J 10 9 4

♠ K Q J 9 4
♡ K 2
◊ A 9 6 5
♣ 6 3

The kibitzers laughed and applauded. The great illusionist gave them his elaborate Coliseum bow. Then, as if he were continuing a performance, he said:

"I thank you, gentlemen. And now I am quite willing to let Hot and Cold win their money back, for I undertake to make a contract of Five Diamonds on that hand."

Hot and Cold both burst out laughing and answered as one:

"We're not betting with you any more. You show us."

"With pleasure," said Oferini. "Look, I ruff the Ace of Spades, and lead a small Diamond. East puts on the Ten, and South plays low. East returns a Club, which is won by dummy's Ace, and the Queen of trumps is led. East covers with the King, which is allowed to hold the trick, South again playing low. East's Club return is won by dummy's King, and now two rounds of trumps pick up East's Knave-Seven. But the second round of trumps squeezes West in Spades and Hearts. So the only tricks the defence makes are two of East's trumps."

Amid the salvo of applause this evoked, Hot asked suspiciously:

"Is that your last word Oferini? Or is there a way of preventing the squeeze?"

224

"Of course there is," smiled the magician. "That squeeze was only an illusion."

"Let us try to find the catch," said Cold, eagerly. "When East wins with the Ten of Diamonds, suppose he returns a trump. What then?"

"Which trump?" asked Oferini. "The Seven? I take it with the Nine, and ruff the Nine of Spades. East can still make one trump trick, but that is all. If East returns the Diamond Knave, I make twelve tricks, because the Queen wins, and the King is finessed against. Finally, if East leads the King, South ducks, and I unblock the Queen in dummy. No, there's only one defence against the squeeze. It is for East, to return a Heart on both occasions when he has the lead. That takes out dummy's entry for the squeeze. So Cold was right in the first place. Against best defence the declarer's best play can make no more than ten tricks. Provided always that West makes the opening lead of the Ace of Spades. That is vital to the defence."

* * *

Most of the Little People seemed themselves somewhat dazed by the illusionist's cunning exploitation of bewilderment, but the Nine of Diamonds was enthusiastic.

"Oferini's display was good theatre," he declared, "and for that reason it brought out, as it were into the limelight, the difference, slight at first view, but very real, between the moderately good player and the expert. On many hands their methods do not diverge, but every now and then a deal comes along that presents to the expert a number of points for consideration which the average good player simply does not see at all. Both may reach the same result, though by different methods; but to the expert the experience will have a richness that passes the other by. I have a vivid recollection of just such a deal. I found myself in the declarer's hand, and, by the means we people of the Pack employ to read the minds of humans, I was privileged to listen-in to—"

A MASTER'S SOLILOQUY

(*The Tale of the Nine of Diamonds*)

THE LITTLE GEM OF WIT AND WISDOM THAT I AM GOING TO
relate occurred in the making of a modest contract of Two.
Here are the North-South cards and the bidding:

♠ K 7 3
♡ A 5 3
◇ A Q
♣ J 6 5 4 3

```
        N
    W       E
        S
```

♠ 9 8 6 5 4
♡ K J 4 2
◇ 9
♣ Q 9 2

North	South
1 ♣	1 ♠
2 ♠	No bid

West led the Queen of trumps. The declarer sagaciously
ducked in dummy, and East took the trick with the Ace.
He led the King of Clubs, and West, void in the suit, discarded a small Diamond. West discarded another small
Diamond on East's Ace of Clubs, and then ruffed the third
round of Clubs with the Deuce. West led the Knave of
trumps, and dummy's King made, East discarding a small
Diamond. These were now the North-South hands:

```
        ♠ 7
        ♡ A 5 3
        ◇ A Q
        ♣ J 6

            N
        W       E
            S

        ♠ 9 8 6
        ♡ K J 4 2
        ◇ 9
        ♣ None
```

So far declarer had lost four tricks, and West still had the Ten of trumps. I watched his mind at work on the problem. He was saying to himself:

"I have two certain trump tricks, two Hearts, one Diamond, and a Club. That's six tricks, and I already have one Spade trick, making seven. Where's the eighth to come from? The Queen of Diamonds and the Heart Knave are candidates. One of two finesses, but if the first one I try goes wrong, I'm sunk. Which should I try first? Or is there a way of avoiding finessing?

"What about a squeeze? If one finesse is right and the other wrong that means both the Diamond King and the Heart Queen will be in the same hand. Then a squeeze would work. I lead a trump to West's Ten. He comes back a Diamond, which dummy's Ace takes. I cash dummy's Knave of Clubs, discarding a small Heart from my hand. Then I ruff the Club Six, and my last trump will squeeze whichever hand holds the Diamond King and guarded Heart Queen, for at that moment dummy will have the Diamond Queen and the Ace and Five of Hearts, while in my hand there'll be the King-Knave-Four of Hearts.

"A pretty piece of play. But if the two critical cards are in different hands, I shall go down that way. And what is more, I shall go down even if both finesses are right. What a fool I'd look, going down when any palooka would make the hand by taking either finesse! Of course, if both finesses are wrong, with the Diamond Queen fully guarded, the contract can't be made, so I needn't worry about that. But surely I can find a way to land the contract in any other case—a way that will get rid of the risk of finessing. Yes, I have it!"

He led the Knave of Clubs from dummy, and discarded me on it from his hand, thus making his hand void of Diamonds. West rightly declined to ruff, so dummy's last trump was led. West's Ten took it, and he returned a Diamond. The Queen was finessed successfully, and two Hearts were discarded on the Queen and Ace of Diamonds. The contract was thus made. As West had no more Spades or Clubs, his only other return would have been a Heart up to South's King-Knave, and again the contract would have been made.

But note that the declarer's claim to meet all cases with the discard of me, except the one where the contract is unmakable, was no vain boast. If East has the two critical cards, he covers the Diamond Queen. South ruffs; cashes his last trump, discarding a small Heart from dummy; then he cashes dummy's Heart Ace and Diamond Ace, and East is squeezed between dummy's Club and South's Heart. If he throws a Club, dummy's Club Six is good; if he throws a Heart, he unguards his Queen.

There remains the case where West has the Heart Queen doubleton, and East the Diamond King. As before East covers dummy's Diamond Queen and South ruffs; cashes his last trump; enters dummy with the Ace of Hearts, and cashes the Ace of Diamonds. At this moment dummy has the Club Six and a small Heart, and East still has a high Club. As East must have had four Hearts if West has only two, East will have already discarded two Hearts, and followed with a third when dummy's Ace of Hearts was played. West, too, will have followed once to Hearts. So the declarer will have seen four of the missing six Hearts. The declarer now plays dummy's last small Heart. When East follows, but not with the Queen, the declarer, who knows East's last card is the high Club, knows also that the Queen of Hearts is bare in West's hand. So he drops it by playing the King, and the Knave of Hearts makes the last trick.

Thus you see that while, with the cards as they actually lay—West having the Diamond King—anyone could have made the contract simply by taking the Diamond finesse, the master who held me played in such a way as to rob that finesse of all risk, and made sure of making his contract if it was makeable at all. He accomplished that by the neat device of discarding me on the Knave of Clubs.

The Diamond Nine's adventure was well received, and as the shrill sounds of approbation swelled and died away, the Queen of Clubs remarked:

"You may wonder at our enthusiasm, Master Robert, but, you see, being handled by experts is our one real pleasure. So much of our time is spent in being played out in obvious ways by the mediocre and the bunglers — winning or losing for them in dull, undistinguished series of games and rubbers."

"Yes," said the Seven of Diamonds; "it would have been poor sort of fun for my brother, the Nine, merely to have been used to take the finesse against the King and land the contract in that flat-footed fashion. We of the Pack, who have to endure so much unintelligent finessing, can share vicariously in the Nine's thrill when he was made the instrument of a piece of play that so ingeniously covered every position of the opposing cards except that about which there was just nothing to be done. You've no idea, Master Robert, what a relief it is for us to find ourselves in the grasp of a man or woman who knows when to finesse and when to squeeze and when to do neither but something else. So many people know expert plays, but only the expert uses them at the right time."

"Which," interposed the Eight of Hearts, "like most sweeping statements, is simply not true. Let me give you a case in point, though I'll admit it's highly exceptional, and that the Diamond Seven is right by and large. The story is rather a sad one, for I was the innocent means of ruining as a bridge player a young man who gave every promise of becoming first-rate. It is only too easy to find a title, for what I assisted at was the—"

BIRTH OF AN IDEE FIXE

(*The Tale of the Eight of Hearts*)

YOUNG MARMADUKE HADDLE HAD NOT YET ATTRACTED THE
attention of the best players in the club. He was keen; his
idea of the game was sound; he had already reached the
stage when he was able to cope with the ordinary run of
hands without making gifts to opponents; he possessed more

knowledge of technique than he had experience to apply it. In short, he was an aspirant to the expert class, though as yet far short of it; and until that fateful day I tell of, when he cut Professor Hardacre as partner, he was on the right road.

It happened that they had rarely cut together before, and the Professor found he had no particular recollection of his young vis-a-vis, except that he had not classified him among the youth who spent most of their time at the table in bluff bidding and false-carding. Marmaduke, for his part, had a great admiration for the Professor's analytical powers, and was eager to acquit himself well.

During the first two or three hands Professor Hardacre mentioned approvingly to himself that "young Haddle shows undoubted signs of ability." Then, in the third game of rubber, Marmaduke dealt thus:

♠ A 7 5 4 3
♡ None
♦ 8 5 4 2
♣ J 8 6 2

♠ J 9 8 6 2
♡ 10 9 7 4
♦ K 10
♣ Q 7

N
W   E
S

♠ None
♡ A J 6 5 3
♦ J 9 7 3
♣ 10 9 5 3

♠ K Q 10
♡ K Q 8 2
♦ A Q 6
♣ A K 4

Marmaduke opened the bidding on the South hand with a conventional Two Clubs; received the negative response of Two Diamonds; and after nibbling at a slam, closed the bidding with Five No-Trumps. West led the Ten of Hearts, and East's Ace took the trick, dummy discarding a Diamond. East returned the Trey of Hearts to South's Queen, dummy throwing another Diamond. Marmaduke then led the King of Spades, and East showed out, discarding the Three of Diamonds.

Feeling rather unhappy, Marmaduke went bravely on and cashed the Ace and King of Clubs, dropping West's Queen. Marmaduke's face brightened, and he surveyed the situation, which now was:

```
                  ♠ A 7 5 4
                  ♡ None
                  ◇ 8 5
                  ♣ J 8
      ♠ J 9 8 6        N        ♠ None
      ♡ 9 7                     ♡ J 6 5
      ◇ K 10       W     E      ◇ J 9 7
      ♣ None           S        ♣ 10 9
                  ♠ Q 10
                  ♡ K 8
                  ◇ A Q 6
                  ♣ 4
```

With four tricks already to his credit, and five others certain, making only nine out of the desired eleven, Marmaduke told himself that his predicament called for some desperate effort. So, after counting up that West had started

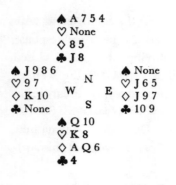

♠ A 7 5 4
♡ None
♢ 8 5
♣ J 8

♠ J 9 8 6   ♠ None
♡ 9 7   ♡ J 6 5
♢ K 10   ♢ J 9 7
♣ None   ♣ 10 9

♠ Q 10
♡ K 8
♢ A Q 6
♣ 4

with five Spades and two Clubs, and might well have had four Hearts, he decided to play West for the doubleton King of Diamonds, and he cashed the Ace of that suit. A good move this—I have said young Haddle had the makings of a real player— and Professor Hardacre nodded his satisfaction.

West just hated that play of the Diamond Ace. He saw himself thrown in with the King, and forced to lead either a Spade, which meant the certain present of a trick to the declarer, or a Heart, which quite probably, he thought, might also be a present. So West exited by throwing his King on South's Ace; and the delighted Marmaduke could now see ten tricks—two Spades, a Heart, a Diamond, and a Club, plus the five tricks he had already taken.

Could he create the eleventh in any way? He came to the conclusion that he couldn't, and made up his mind to take his certain tricks, and be one down. That wouldn't disgrace him in Professor Hardacre's eyes. Surely he'd done well enough by dropping the Queen of Clubs and forcing West to make the Queen of Diamonds good when a finesse would have failed. At this moment his intention was to cash the Queen of Spades, but accidentally he took hold of me instead, and played me. West promptly covered me with the Nine.

It was then that Marmaduke noticed what he had done. But he gave no sign of his inadvertence, as he thought it did not matter: the Eight of Hearts was a loser, anyway. So he quietly discarded a Spade from the table, and East played low, leaving the lead with West, who returned his last Heart. Dummy threw another Spade, and South's King took the trick. Marmaduke now reverted to his original intention, and cashed his two Spade tricks. To his astonishment, he found that in so doing he had squeezed East in Diamonds and Clubs. After much thought, East threw a Diamond, and Marmaduke made the last two tricks in that suit.

All would have been well, if Professor Hardacre had not been his partner. Anyone else would probably have said: "Well played, partner!" and that would have been that. Not thus Professor Hardacre. He was a kindly man and generous, and analysis was his joy.

"Bravo, young man!" he cried. "You played that hand brilliantly. Your lead of the Eight of Hearts at the seventh trick was masterly. If you had played any other card, your opponents could have evaded the squeeze. To bring off the squeeze, you had first to lose a trick, and it had to be at that moment. Your sense of timing was colossal. For you realised, of course, that you had to keep the Heart Eight until then in case West had not thrown his King under your Ace of Diamonds. The Eight of Hearts is then a menace card against East or West, according to which Heart West returns when you throw him in with the King of Diamonds. He can't play a Spade, of course, as that gives you the contract at once. If he leads the Nine of Hearts, that leaves the duty of protecting the Heart suit with East, who would be squeezed be-

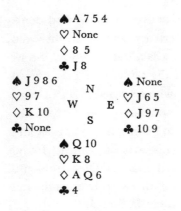

```
                ♠ A 7 5 4
                ♡ None
                ◇ 8 5
                ♣ J 8
  ♠ J 9 8 6              ♠ None
  ♡ 9 7         N        ♡ J 6 5
  ◇ K 10    W      E     ◇ J 9 7
  ♣ None        S        ♣ 10 9
                ♠ Q 10
                ♡ K 8
                ◇ A Q 6
                ♣ 4
```

tween Hearts and Clubs. If West leads the Seven of Hearts, that destroys East's Heart protection, and it is now West who would be squeezed between Spades and Hearts. You would, of course, discard from dummy according to the needs of the situation. If West leads the Nine of Hearts, dummy's discard is a Spade; if West leads the Seven, dummy discards a Club. But in either case, note the importance of the Eight of Hearts as the menace card. And the same card, the Heart Eight, is the only card that can be used to lose a trick in the play as it actually went, as you have so conclusively demonstrated. The hand is a veritable rhapsody of squeezes, and I congratulate you on the convincing way you read the distribution of opponents' hands and controlled a situation that positively bristled with difficulties."

Well, after that, is there any human being who would have admitted that his play of me was a slip of the hand? All Marmaduke could do was to mutter his thanks to the Professor. But it was the end of him as a bridge player. From that moment—and who can wonder at it?—poor Marmaduke became a squeeze-addict. In practically every hand he plays as declarer he looks for a squeeze and plays for a squeeze. He simply cannot take a finesse, except in trumps. If there are nine tricks on top in Three No-Trumps, he tries to plan a squeeze for an overtrick, and loses the contract. He hardly ever comes to the club. He has lost too much, and now frequents small clubs where they play for trifling stakes, and where his unhappy mania costs him little. I warned you it was a sad story.

*　　*　　*

The Eight of Hearts concluding remark had been drawn from him by the sight of the woebegone faces of his companions. The tender-hearted little creatures seemed really upset over Marmaduke's fate. I hastened to say what I could to comfort them. It was true, I told them, that I hadn't seen young Haddle in the club for some time; and I promised I would make a point of searching him out in his new haunts and do what I could to effect a cure.

They cheered up at that, after thanking me charmingly in chorus. Then said the Knave of Spades:

"As one who has made modern psychology his hobby, may I venture to suggest, Master Robert, that the best line of treatment to adopt with young Marmaduke is not to make a frontal attack on his obsession, but to try to interest him in some other method of play than squeezes, and preferably a method that crops up frequently."

"What about finessing?" put in the Ten of Hearts. "That's frequent enough, goodness knows."

"I don't see why not," replied the Spade Knave. "We've all been talking rather disparagingly about finessing. I know it is almost the only expert play the average human can execute, and that the indifferent player always takes every finesse within sight. But let us free ourselves from cant. Finessing is an integral part of the game; and if you, Master

Robert, can convince your patient that the finesse can sometimes be as spectacular and as sure a sign of sound analysis as the most erudite end-play, you may well succeed in curing him."

"In that case," said the Nine of Clubs, "I can furnish Master Robert with an excellent hand for him to use in introducing the subject to poor Haddle. I think I may fairly term it—"

A STUDY IN FINESSING

(*The Tale of the Nine of Clubs*)

PERHAPS YOU WOULDN'T MIND TELLING A WHITE LIE,
Master Robert, by letting Marmaduke think his idol, Professor Hardacre, played the hand. Actually, it would be
only half a white lie, for the Professor was appealed to in

the post-mortem. Anyway, the declarer was an expert all right, and the Professor definitely came down on his side. Here are the North-South hands and the bidding:

$$
\begin{array}{l}
\spadesuit \; A\,3\,2 \\
\heartsuit \; K\,2 \\
\diamondsuit \; 6\,5\,4\,3\,2 \\
\clubsuit \; A\,8\,2
\end{array}
$$

```
        N
    W       E
        S
```

$$
\begin{array}{l}
\spadesuit \; 5\,4 \\
\heartsuit \; A\,J\,4\,3 \\
\diamondsuit \; A \\
\clubsuit \; K\,Q\,J\,10\,7\,6
\end{array}
$$

SOUTH	NORTH
1 ♣	2 N-T
3 ♡	4 ♣
4 N-T (Blackwood)	5 ♡
6 ♣	7 ♣

West chose the most awkward lead for the declarer of the King of Spades. South considered the two hands for quite a while—as well he might. Then he took the trick with dummy's Ace and led the Deuce of Hearts. East played low, and South finessed with the Knave, which held the trick. He then cashed the Ace of Diamonds, and led the Seven of trumps. West played the Five, and the declarer finessed by putting on dummy's Eight. East eagerly produced me, and the contract was defeated.

242

North, who no doubt was painfully conscious he had overbid his hand, took the offensive in the post-mortem by snorting at his partner and exclaiming:

"I've never seen such reckless play in all my life! Fancy finessing right and left like that at the very outset of a Grand Slam hand!"

South warmly defended himself.

"My play was the only possible way of landing the contract," he declared.

"What!" ejaculated North. "Do you mean to tell me you had to finesse against the Nine of trumps on the first round with nine trumps in our two hands?"

"I'm telling you just that," returned South. "I had to find a parking place for my losing Spade. There is no imaginable squeeze, and nowhere for that losing Spade to go except on dummy's fifth Diamond. For that to happen, the opponent's trumps must be drawn, and the Diamonds must be ruffed three times. That calls for three entries into dummy. A fourth entry is needed to cash dummy's fifth Diamond when it is established. These four entries to dummy can only be the King of Hearts and the three trumps, since the opening lead has taken out the Ace of Spades. The Ace and Eight of trumps must be used as entries in the course of drawing opponents' trumps, and the Deuce of Clubs must be kept to ruff a Heart and at the same time act as the entry for cashing the established long Diamond. It is thus clear that the hand must be played on the assumption that the adverse trumps are divided 2-2, and that West holds the Nine, enabling the Eight to be finessed. In that case, as the Heart finesse had already succeeded, the play would have gone:

♠ A 3 2
♡ K 2
◇ 6 5 4 3 2
♣ A 8 2

```
      N
   W     E
      S
```

♠ 5 4
♡ A J 4 3
◇ A
♣ K Q J 10 7 6

First trick, Spade Ace; second trick, Heart finesse; third trick, Diamond Ace; fourth trick, Club Eight finesse; fifth trick, Diamond ruff; sixth trick, Club Ace; seventh trick, Diamond ruff; eighth trick, Heart King; ninth trick, Diamond ruff; tenth trick, Heart ruff; eleventh trick, dummy's fifth Diamond, on which South discards his losing Spade; twelfth trick, one of dummy's Spades ruffed in South's hand; and South's Ace of Hearts makes the thirteenth trick. That is how I planned it; but as East turned up with the trump Nine, the contract was unmakeable, and I defy you to land it by any line of play."

After a few moments' thought North grunted reluctant acquiescence.

"I suppose you're right there," he said. "But I see no justification for your Heart finesse, although it worked. Surely it would have been better to play out the Ace and King, and try to drop the Queen with the third-round ruff."

"I don't agree," said South, firmly. "I think the finesse is the better chance. But as it is purely a question of mathematics, let us put it to Professor Hardacre. He's playing at that table across the room."

They waited till Professor was dummy, and then they got from him the lecture they knew was inevitable.

"Should you finesse or should you play for the third-round drop of the Queen? Well, let us analyse the chances.

Both the drop and the finesse win if East has the Queen singleton, doubleton, or trebleton. Both plays lose if West has four or more cards to the Queen, or if East has all the missing Hearts. Now let us compare the cases where only one way wins and the other loses, as these are the only cases that matter."

The Professor took a scoring pad, and wrote on it:

Finesse alone wins if		Drop alone wins if	
West has:	East has:	West has:	East has:
x.	Q.x.x.x.x.x	Q	x.x.x.x.x.x
x.x	Q.x.x.x.x	Q.x	x.x.x.x.x
x.x.x	Q.x.x.x	Q.x.x	x.x.x.x

"So you see, gentlemen, the critical cases occur at the same suit lengths. The sole question is whether the Queen is in the West or East hand. Well, you notice how numerous are the cards attending her when she is with East and how few when she is with West. If you did not know in which of two unequal groups a person you were seeking was, would not the probabilities be in favour of finding him or her in the larger group? It is simple, in the case you have submitted to me, to work out the chances in percentage. To be exact, the probabilities are 61.6 per cent. in favour of the finesse—that is, of the Queen being in the larger group—and 38.4 per cent, for the drop—that is for her being in the smaller group. So the declarer was right to finesse in preference to playing for the drop."

*　　*　　*

"That's the stuff!" said the King of Hearts. "Get Marmaduke bitten with percentage play, and he'll regain his sanity all right. There's nothing healthier or more profitable for bridge players. A trifle on the dull side, perhaps, but that's all to the good when you are trying to wean a squeeze-addict from his hectic course. The very contrast in the cool calculation of probabilities may appeal to him. But I do hope we've not been boring *you,* Master Robert. I'm afraid you may have found the detailed analyses of the last few hands rather wearisome."

"Not at all," I replied. "And anyway to have a certain number of closely analysed hands will give variety to the book."

"What book?" came in chorus from the Wee Folk.

"Well," I told them, "it didn't take me long to realise that in entertaining me so kindly with your tales, you were presenting me with some wonderful material for a book. You took that risk with your eyes open, for you knew I was a writer, and writers are omnivorous and unscrupulous. I hope none of you mind, but your stories are enthralling me, and I intend to pass them on to other bridge players in your very words, as well as I can remember them."

I need not have doubted. The tiny creatures were plainly delighted at the notion, and exchanged glances of satisfaction and pleased nudges. The Ace of Spades spoke for the Pack.

"We had rather hoped we were giving you some useful material for your writing, Master Robert," he said. "But we had not thought of your making a book of us and our tales. We are happy to think that bridge players will be told of our existence, even though but a few of them will ever see us and quite a number of them will disbelieve that you ever did."

"That will be their loss," broke in the King of Clubs. "For though I say it but shouldn't, we *are* nice to know, we People of the Pack, and the bridge player is fortunate who has us on his side, as some of the incidents we have told you go to show. But, of course, there are people who don't know what is good even when it's under their noses. In the adventure I am adding to your collection, Master Robert, one partner saw the light, and the other didn't. Fortunately, the blind one was unable to interfere and so he was—"

SAVED DESPITE HIMSELF

(*The Tale of the King of Clubs*)

WE KINGS LIKE TO PLAY A STRENUOUS PART IN THE FIGHT.
It gives us small pleasure to be guarded and cosseted like
battleships. Which is why I remember so gratefully the
player who directed me in the play of this slam contract:

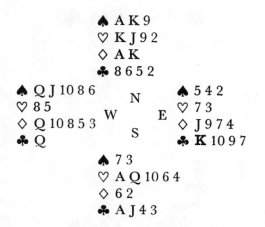

       ♠ A K 9
       ♡ K J 9 2
       ◇ A K
       ♣ 8 6 5 2

♠ Q J 10 8 6   ♠ 5 4 2
♡ 8 5   ♡ 7 3
◇ Q 10 8 5 3   ◇ J 9 7 4
♣ Q   ♣ K 10 9 7

       ♠ 7 3
       ♡ A Q 10 6 4
       ◇ 6 2
       ♣ A J 4 3

With both sides vulnerable the bidding went:

SOUTH	NORTH
1 ♡	3 ♡
4 ♡	4 N-T (Blackwood)
5 ♡	6 ♡

West started off with the Queen of Spades, taken by
dummy's King. The declarer drew trumps in two rounds;
cashed dummy's Spade Ace and ruffed dummy's last Spade;
cashed the Ace and King of Diamonds; and led dummy's
Deuce of Clubs.

My man, East, considered a moment. Then, to my joy,
he launched me into the thick of the fight. I made things
happen, I can tell you. South put on his Ace, and West,
with a spasm of annoyance distorting his face, was compelled to drop the Queen on the trick. South looked pleased
at his catch. But not for long. He led a small Club. East

took it, and returned another Club. Now nothing could prevent East from making a second Club trick.

Was West satisfied with the result? Not at all.

"We'd have got them down two tricks, partner," he complained, "if you had played low to the first Club trick, for then I should probably have made my Queen."

"You would, indeed," said East. "For South would have played low, too. Then you would have had to return either a Spade or a Diamond, of which suits the North-South hands had been stripped. So the declarer would have ruffed in dummy, and discarded a small Club from South. Then a simple finesse in Clubs against my King would have landed the contract. I'm terribly sorry I hurt your feelings by crashing your Queen, but, you see, I thought it more important to rescue you from the dilemma of the lead and to defeat the slam."

* * *

The Clubs and Diamonds laughed, but the two major tribes were not greatly amused.

"Rather a heavy-handed piece of sarcasm," pronounced the Queen of Hearts, distastefully, "though I suppose West did ask for it."

"Oh, you Hearts and Spades are too fastidious for this work-a-day world," said the Eight of Clubs, impatiently. "Of course, West deserved to be ticked off for not appreciating his partner's good play. The trouble with defence is that unless one of the partners happens to be able to control the situation, as in the tale our gracious King has just told, good defence depends on partnership co-operation. I know of a case in point, where brilliant deceptive play by one partner was rendered of no effect through lack of insight by the other. I would have you entitle my story, Master Robert, with a phrase most players will find poignant—"

A DEADLY ALLY

(*The Tale of the Eight of Clubs*)

THE DEFENDERS IN THIS BRIEF HISTORY DISPLAYED TO-
wards each other that courtesy which some players reserve
for their life outside the bridge club. And, of course, I agree

253

with Her Majesty of the Heart tribe that that is how it should be. But then East was a master, and West was aware of it, and knew he was not. The deal and the bidding:

```
                ♠ Q 6 4
                ♡ A Q 10
                ◇ A K
                ♣ K J 10 6 4
  ♠ J 10 9 5                    ♠ 7 3 2
  ♡ K J 5          N            ♡ 7 4 3 2
  ◇ 7 5 3     W       E         ◇ Q 10 6 4
  ♣ A 9 3          S            ♣ Q 8
                ♠ A K 8
                ♡ 9 8 6
                ◇ J 9 8 2
                ♣ 7 5 2
```

NORTH	SOUTH
1 ♣	1 N-T
4 N-T	No bid

North's Four No-Trumps was not conventional, but a raise in No-Trumps; and South, who felt a slam to be extremely unlikely, was right to pass.

West opened with the Knave of Spades, which South's Ace won. The declarer led the Deuce of Clubs; West played the Trey; dummy's Ten was finessed; and East unhesitantly dropped me on the trick. The declarer returned to the closed hand with the King of Spades, and led the Five of Clubs. West put up the Ace, crashing East's Queen. With the Clubs thus set up, the declarer easily made his contract with four Club tricks, two Diamonds, the Ace of Hearts (he could not get back to his hand to finesse Hearts), and three Spade tricks.

East made no remark at the end of the hand, and was quietly entering up the score. But West felt dimly that something had gone wrong somewhere. Quite diffidently, he said to East:

"You didn't take the first Club trick with your Queen. Wouldn't it have broken the contract if you had?"

"Actually, no, it wouldn't," replied East. "That was why I tried a little bit of bluff by putting on the Eight. My idea was to entice the declarer to return to his hand, thus using up what I suspected would be his last entry, and take the Club finesse again. I intended to make the Queen, if he did that, and return a Spade, taking out dummy's last stopper in the suit. Then, when you got in with the Club Ace, you could have cashed your high Spade, and put dummy on play with a Diamond. In that way you would have made still another trick with your King of Hearts, as the declarer would have been pinned to the table.

"If I had made the first Club trick with the Queen, and returned a Spade, the declarer would have had no further finesse in Clubs to take, and so would have gone at once for the Heart finesse, which I knew was right for him. He would then have played a Club from dummy, drawing your Ace, and would have made his contract, losing only two Clubs and a Heart."

"I see," said West, regretfully; "and I went and spoilt everything by putting up my Ace of Clubs on the second round. When the declarer had fallen into your trap, too.

I had nothing to gain by going in with the Ace, had I? There was no need for hurry, was there?"

"No, you hadn't; and there wasn't," said East smiling amiably.

*　　*　　*

"Well, of course, mishaps like that are bound to happen when the partnership is unequal," remarked the Queen of Diamonds. "If you want to find examples of enterprising, co-operative defence, you must look for them among partners who are of about the same ability and who play the same type of game."

"That's perfectly true, Mam," the Ten of Spades agreed. "One of the most striking defences I was ever concerned in was brought off by a pair who had complete understanding of each other's ways. The first step was taken by one partner in the bidding, and the other carried the matter to a successful conclusion in the play. It was a very model of—"

A PSYCHIC DEFENCE

(*The Tale of the Ten of Spades*)

THEIR PARTNERSHIP DATED BACK SEVERAL YEARS BEFORE
their marriage, which itself was quite recent. He was rather
given to bluff bidding and play, and she, not to be outdone,
claimed and exercised the right to go psychic, too, when she

felt like it. There was nothing subservient about that young woman. But her husband seemed to like it, and, in bridge at any rate, she was justified, for he was only slightly the better player. They combined well, and while their methods were naturally not uniformly successful, most people found them a formidable pair to play against.

She was sitting East and he West. Their opponents had won the first game of the rubber, when North dealt, and bid One Club. She called a Spade, and South went One No-Trumps. West passed, and North tried Two No-Trumps, which South raised to game in No-Trumps. I had been dealt to the husband, West. Here are his cards and dummy's:

```
                    ♠ A J 8
                    ♡ Q 10 3
                    ◇ 5 3
                    ♣ A K 9 5 2
        He                          She
   ♠ Q 10 9 6 4          N
   ♡ 8 6 2                         E
   ◇ Q 8 2          W    S
   ♣ 8 4
```

Before North's cards went down, I caught my man, West saying to himself:

"I've five Spades to the Queen-Ten, and opponents' bidding sounds as if they've each got a Spade stop. Looks to me as if Esther's Spade bid was a psych. If so, I mustn't do anything to help the declarer to get a count on our hands, and discover her bluff. I'd better false-card a bit."

And he led the Six of Hearts, and murmured to himself: "Thought so," when he saw dummy's Ace-Knave-Eight of Spades. Dummy's Three of Hearts was played, and East took the trick with the King. She returned the Ten of Diamonds; South's Knave covered; and West's Queen made. He led back Diamonds, false-carding again with the Deuce. East put on the King. South allowed it to hold the trick, but his Ace made as she continued the suit. The declarer now cashed the Queen and Knave of Clubs from his own hand, and crossed to the table with a third Club. My man, West, kept up his pretence of having a Heart suit by throwing the Heart Eight on the third Club. I noticed he was thinking hard, and I listened-in, and heard:

"The blighter has five sure Club tricks, and he's made the Ace of Diamonds. He's bound to have the King of Spades, and the Ace is in dummy. That's eight tricks. Where will he go for the ninth? He daren't try to set up a Heart trick, because if we make one more Diamond trick, we defeat him. So he'll just have to go after a Spade trick, and as the Knave's in dummy, he has only a one-way finesse into Esther's hand. Despite her Spade bid, he'll have to try it, as he has no other way to play. He won't like doing it, but he'll just have to. Well, I think I'll just relieve his mind of some of the worry."

So when the declarer led the fourth Club from dummy, West quietly threw on it the Nine of Spades; and followed this up by throwing me on dummy's fifth Club. The declarer's face grew happy, as he realised that dummy's Knave and Eight of Spades had become equals, and that he now could finesse Spades either way. So he confidently led the

Knave of Spades from dummy to finesse through the hand that had bid Spades. He made no more tricks. West's Spade Queen took the Knave, and a Heart lead to East's Ace enabled her to cash the last two Diamonds. The declarer was thus three tricks down.

"Well played, Tom," said Esther.

"I should jolly well think it was well played," Tom replied eagerly. "Did you see how I—"

"Yes, I saw," said Esther, firmly.

Tom subsided.

*　　*　　*

The Little People plainly relished the young couple's triumph, and the Knave of Clubs exclaimed:

"What joy to break a perfectly good contract by such piquant guile sustained throughout the bidding and play! That's co-operative defence all right, that is!"

Here the tiny Two of Hearts began to giggle. They all turned to look at him.

"I'll tell you of a co-operative defence," he laughed. "The Knaves won't be pleased to hear it was completely guileless, but it achieved its objective one hundred per cent. There never was such a defence in the whole history of bridge, and I don't suppose there ever will be again. I hope I'm not giving the show away when I call it—"

A CHIVALROUS CONSPIRACY

(*The Tale of the Two of Hearts*)

IT WAS A COUNTRY HOUSE PARTY, AND ONE AFTERNOON, when pouring rain kept them indoors, two boys and two girls sat down to play bridge. They were sweethearts, but in the modern fashion, which meant they bickered and fought and flung at each other endearing and abusive terms alternately.

They pivotted as partners, and for some time the play was fast and feverish, but with no great damage done to anybody's pocket-money. Then the boys played against the girls, and held the better cards. The boys won a game. The girls declined to let them have the rubber, and were about a thousand to the bad above the line in penalties, when these hands were dealt with the boys sitting East-West:

Miss North
♠ 10 8 6
♡ 9
♢ 9 8 7 6 5 4 3 2
♣ 9

♠ K J 9 7   **N**   ♠ A Q
♡ 8   ♡ A K Q J 7 5 3
♢ K 10   **W**   **E**   ♢ A Q J
♣ A K Q 8 6 4   **S**   ♣ 10

♠ 5 4 3 2
♡ 10 6 4 2
♢ None
♣ J 7 5 3 2
Betty South

The East-West cards have a Grand Slam in any denomination, and although little Miss North, who had dealt, valiantly opened the bidding with Three Diamonds, the boys rapidly bid to Seven Hearts, declared by East. This was more than Betty South could bear, and before she realised it, she had wrathfully announced:

"Seven No-Trumps!"

West doubled, and to him Miss North scornfully addressed herself.

"How brave of you to double," she sneered. "What courage, what resource! Why, you know I haven't a single high card, and I'd be surprised if Betty has either. Go on, mark us

262

thirteen tricks down, heroic little fellows that you are!"

The two boys glanced at each other across the table. Then West said to Miss North:

"We won't take any tricks we haven't earned. The hand must be played out."

"But I can't make a single trick," said Betty South.

"You never know, darling," East told her. "It's astonishing what can happen."

The boys exchanged another look, and I caught the hint of a wink passed forth and back.

"Oh, well, hurry up and get it over," said Betty rather crossly.

West led the Eight of Clubs, and Betty, astonished, made her Knave. She looked right and left at the two boys, but their faces were serene and studiously blank. Wonderingly she led the Seven of Clubs, and discarded a Diamond from dummy, while West carefully underplayed with the Six of Clubs and East showed out, discarding his Ace of Spades.

Then she knew what they were up to. A dimple stole out in one cheek, and there just reached me her murmur:

"The lambs! How idiotically divine of them!"

She now led her Five of Clubs, but this time, when West played the Four, she was careful to rid dummy of the Spade Six. She could play the cards, could Miss Betty! East discarded the Queen of Spades. Knowing West could not underplay Clubs any longer, Betty switched to Spades, leading the Deuce. West played the Seven, and dummy's Eight made, East taking the opportunity to discard his Ace of Hearts. Dummy's lead of the Ten of Spades was underplayed by West with the Nine, after East had thrown the

```
              Miss North
              ♠ 10 8 6
              ♡ 9
              ◇ 9 8 7 6 5 4 3 2
              ♣ 9
♠ K J 9 7                        ♠ A Q
♡ 8              N               ♡ A K Q J 7 5 3
◇ K 10      W       E            ◇ A Q J
♣ A K Q 8 6 4   S               ♣ 10
              ♠ 5 4 3 2
              ♡ 10 6 4 2
              ◇ None
              ♣ J 7 5 3 2
              Betty South
```

King of Hearts, and South followed with the Three of Spades.

Now Betty led dummy's Nine of Hearts. East played the Seven, and Betty overtook with her Ten, West's Eight falling to the trick. On Betty's lead of the Six of Hearts West got rid of his King of Spades, while East underplayed with the Heart Five. On Betty's Heart Four West's Knave of Spades was thrown, and East still had the Heart Three with which to underplay.

At this stage Betty cashed the Four and Five of Spades, on which West threw his Ace and King of Clubs, and East the Queen and Knave of Hearts. That made me the highest of my tribe. Betty cashed me, which enabled West to discard his last Club, the Queen. Betty's last two Clubs were now tricks.

So she made her Grand Slam, doubled, amid scenes of hilarity that bordered on the hysterical, especially at tricks nine and ten, when both boys were industriously discarding Court personages on Betty's low Spades. When calm was restored, it was only momentary. For Miss North was heard to ask of herself musingly:

"Why *didn't* I think of redoubling?"

This was just a bit too much for the boys; but the rough-house that ensued is not for your book, I think, Master Robert.

* * *

The light-hearted escapade drew tremendous applause, and as it died down, the Ace of Diamonds exclaimed:

"Betty South's discard of the Six of Spades at the third trick must be a quite unique kind of unblocking, for it was necessary to allow West—an opponent—time to get rid of his two high Spades. That child has the makings of a master to have seen the need for this play in such unusual circumstances."

The Eight of Clubs went off on another tack.

"The Queen of Diamonds asked for examples of co-operative defence," he chuckled. "I hope she's satisfied with that one."

"Indeed I am," smiled that fair beauty, "and glad too, to know that chivalry still lives—even at the bridge table."

"All the same," interposed the Queen of Spades, in dignified fashion, "it is the chivalry and the technique that were unusual in that pleasing tale, not the fact that the defence helped the declarer. That happens often, though naturally the aid is given either unwillingly or unwittingly. In one exploit in which I took part the declarer actually compelled both defenders to present him with tricks. I cherish the memory for that reason and also because the declarer's play showed proper realisation of the importance of us high personages of the Pack. I was neither squandered in uselessly covering one of the lower honours, nor was I given the merely routine task of trick-taking. I was reserved for the crucial play that resulted in—"

265

A DOUBLE ELIMINATION

(*The Tale of the Queen of Spades*)

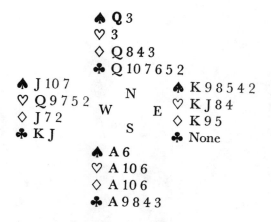

♠ Q 3
♡ 3
◇ Q 8 4 3
♣ Q 10 7 6 5 2

♠ J 10 7   ♠ K 9 8 5 4 2
♡ Q 9 7 5 2   ♡ K J 8 4
◇ J 7 2   ◇ K 9 5
♣ K J   ♣ None

♠ A 6
♡ A 10 6
◇ A 10 6
♣ A 9 8 4 3

The precise course of the bidding does not matter. North-South reached a contract of Five Clubs, with South as declarer. In the early stages East had twice bid Spades, and West's opening lead was the Knave of that suit.

At the outset the declarer had the intelligence to perceive that, unless the King of trumps was going to drop on the Ace, the contract could be made only by throw-in play, in which case I should be needed to steer the lead into East's hand. He therefore did not waste the power of my personality on covering the Knave in the faint hope that West had played the Knave from King-Knave. He put on dummy's Trey, and took the trick with the Ace in his own hand.

He now set about the preliminary work of stripping the North-South hands of Hearts and Spades. He cashed his Ace of Hearts, and ruffed a Heart in dummy. Returning to his hand with the Ace of Clubs, he learned that he had to lose a trump trick to the King, and felt gratified that he had planned his play in anticipation of that possibility.

After ruffing his last Heart in dummy, he led me, thus saddling East with the lead, when he took the trick with his King. East did not relish the situation. He dared not give the declarer a ruff-and-discard by returning either a Spade or a Heart, so he had to play away from his King of Diamonds, and chose to lead the Nine. South covered with the Ten; West put on the Knave; and dummy's Queen made.

A Club lead from the table put West on play in his turn. He, too, was in a dilemma. A Heart or Spade from him would again have allowed the declarer to ruff in dummy and discard a Diamond from his hand. So he, too, led a Diamond. But the first round of Diamonds had in no whit robbed the North-South hands of their tenace holding in that suit, and whether West led the Seven or the Deuce, the declarer must make two more tricks in Diamonds and his contract. Actually, West led the Seven, which was covered by dummy's Eight. East played the King, and South's Ace and Six made.

Now observe what would have happened if the declarer had used me to cover the Knave in the first trick. West would have made a trick with his Ten of Spades, and would have cashed the King of trumps. He would then have led a Diamond, but after that neither East nor West could have been thrown in again to lead Diamonds, and the declarer must lose one trick in that suit.

Note, too, that it was also necessary for the declarer to give the lead to East by playing me before throwing West into play. For if the declarer first threw West in with the King of Clubs, West could get rid of the lead with a Spade, and again the defence would have been compelled only once to lead Diamonds. Thus the declarer had to realise not only my importance for throwing the lead to East, but also the importance of playing me at precisely the right moment.

The lower values among the Wee Folk had grown restive under the Spade Queen's bombastic manner, and the Five of Clubs called out:

"Your tremendously important task, Mam, of placing the lead with East was equalled by one of us little Clubs, who threw the lead to West."

"Yes," replied the Queen, her handsome dark eyes flashing disdain, "any one of you small fry did for that, but only a high personage could control the placing of the lead in Spades."

Angry murmurs came from the smaller creatures, and I feared another violent outbreak of the ancient quarrel. But the Two of Diamonds, his minute face crimson with fury, saved the situation.

"I'll cap Your Majesty's story," he fumed, "with another which will prove beyond any denial that in this wondrous game of bridge there are times when high personages are of no account and we 'smaller fry' take over your functions. We do not deny your power, but we do demand recognition of our worth. In a much more complicated and unusual situation than that Your Majesty has told of, I played an infinitely more important part then the one you have so proudly related. It was a rare case of—"

A DEUCE IN A DUAL ROLE

(The Tale of the Two of Diamonds)

<small>UNLIKE THE SPADE QUEEN'S TALE, DETAILS OF THE BIDDING</small>
cannot be omitted from mine, for they enabled the declarer

to plan his play. North-South only were vulnerable, when these hands were dealt:

```
                    ♠ A K J 8 2
                    ♡ 10 6 5 2
                    ◊ 7 5
                    ♣ 5 3
   ♠ Q 10 9 6              N              ♠ 7 5 4 3
   ♡ 4                                    ♡ J 8 7 3
   ◊ A K 6        W          E            ◊ J 10 9 3
   ♣ K Q J 9 2           S               ♣ 10
                    ♠ None
                    ♡ A K Q 9
                    ◊ Q 8 4 2
                    ♣ A 8 7 6 4
```

SOUTH	WEST	NORTH	EAST
1 ♣	Double	No bid	1 ◊
1 ♡	1 ♠	Double	No bid
No bid	2 ♣	No bid	No bid
Double	No bid	2 ♡	No bid
3 ♡	No bid	4 ♡	No bid
No bid	No bid		

West could easily have defeated the contract by leading the King of Clubs, but he made the mistake of starting off with Diamonds, and this gave the declarer an opportunity of which, slight as it was, he availed himself to the full. On the King and Ace of Diamonds East played the Knave and Nine and South the Four and Eight. West then shifted, too late, to the King of Clubs, which South's Ace took.

The declarer, in possession of the field, began drawing trumps, but when West discarded the Deuce of Clubs on the second round, the declarer paused to reconsider the situation, which now was:

```
                  ♠ A K J 8 2
                  ♡ 10 6
                  ◇ None
                  ♣ 5
   ♠ Q 10 9 6           N        ♠ 7 5 4 3
   ♡ None          W        E    ♡ J 8
   ◇ 6                  S        ◇ 10 3
   ♣ Q J 9                       ♣ None
                  ♠ None
                  ♡ Q 9
                  ◇ Q 2
                  ♣ 8 7 6 4
```

West's bid of Clubs showed he had five, so the declarer knew East must now be void of the suit. So far the declarer had taken three tricks—two trumps and a Club. He could see two more trump tricks, a Diamond, a Diamond ruff, and two Spades—making nine in all. He set to work to create the tenth trick.

With seeming perversity, he began by giving up one of his sure tricks. He ruffed the Queen of Diamonds in dummy with the Ten. Then he led the Six of trumps, and finessed with the Nine when East put on the Eight. The Queen of Hearts drew East's last trump. On the two rounds of trumps West threw two Clubs, and dummy the Deuce of Spades.

It was at this moment that the declarer sent me forth with

a two-fold mission. First, I acted as a squeeze card on West, who had either to throw his last Club, making South's Clubs good, or shorten his Spade defence. He chose to let go the Six of Spades. Secondly, I gave the lead to East, who had to take me with his bare Ten.

Now declarer held his breath with anxiety. Would his ingenious plan work? He knew East had only Spades to lead, but did he or did he not have the Nine among his four Spades? If he did, and led a small Spade, the contract could not be made. The declarer had been compelled to bank on West having the Queen-Ten-Nine for his Spade bid. Also he knew East must be very weak in high cards, or he would have bid one of his four-card majors in response to his partner's take-out double in preference to Diamonds. Still he might have the Spade Nine. But all was well. East did not have the Nine, and his forced Spade lead enabled dummy to make four tricks in Spades and the declarer to fulfil his contract.

And now I would draw the attention of the Queen of Spades to the fact that in this deal I was able to perform a task for which the Queen of Diamonds would have been useless. That high personage—she will know I mean no disrespect when I say this—had to be got rid of by being ruffed, for she could not have thrown the lead to East as I did. I would also ask the Queen of Spades to note that the declarer ruffed the Queen of Diamonds with an honour, and used a small trump, the Six, for the important work of taking the trump finesse. I think you should find the hand interesting, Master Robert, for in ruffing the Queen of Diamonds the declarer had resort to a rare artifice—that of reducing the high-card value of his Diamond holding. But I claim that I have completely answered the Queen of Spades, for if ever there was a case of small cards proving of greater usefulness than high cards, it is this hand.

*　　*　　*

The Diamond Two's voice ended on a note of shrill triumph, and all eyes turned towards the Queen of Spades. But that proud lady held a scornful silence, head in air. When it became evident that she did not intend to reply, the smaller creatures gave a vigorous burst of applause to mark their satisfaction. With suave diplomacy, the Ace of Diamonds intervened. Giving his Deuce a congratulatory pat, he said:

"That was a fine hand indeed, my lad, to add to Master Robert's collection—a remarkable example of the values you smaller folk can assume in the intricate manoeuvres of the modern game. We honours have long since learned that it quite frequently turns out that way when expert players handle the cards. If some of us sometimes display a little jealousy at the enhanced status to which you have risen in these days, you should take it as an involuntary compliment. And now, as a contrast, I shall tell of an adventure of mine which was mainly a battle of high cards. At first sight the situation seemed ordinary enough, but in reality success depended on clear thinking by the declarer. It was, as so often—"

A MATTER OF ENTRIES

(*The Tale of the Ace of Diamonds*)

THE HAND OCCURRED IN A MATCH BETWEEN TWO TEAMS. When it was dealt, one of the terms was well ahead. That meant both were taking risks, for the team behind was making every effort to catch up, while their opponents were trying to forestall possible big swings against them by equalising the chances. With both sides vulnerable, North dealt thus:

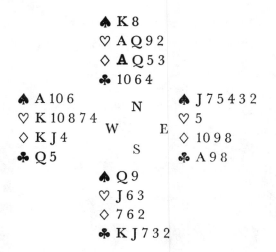

♠ K 8
♡ A Q 9 2
◇ A Q 5 3
♣ 10 6 4

♠ A 10 6
♡ K 10 8 7 4
◇ K J 4
♣ Q 5

N
W   E
S

♠ J 7 5 4 3 2
♡ 5
◇ 10 9 8
♣ A 9 8

♠ Q 9
♡ J 6 3
◇ 7 6 2
♣ K J 7 3 2

The bidding was identical in the two rooms. North opened
with a Diamond; South responded with One No-Trumps;
and North raised to Three No-Trumps. Both Norths were
aware that their values did not justify the jump to game;
but the North in arrears just took the risk, and the other,
suspecting that his opposite number would shoot for nine
tricks, decided to be in the same contract in case it happened
to be there for the making.

In both rooms West led the Seven of Hearts. This was
lucky for the declarers, neither of whom could have made
more than six tricks if Spades had been led. Both declarers
won the trick with South's Knave, as the Eleven Rule
showed that East could have no card higher than the Seven.

Both declarers led another Heart, and won in dummy
with the Nine. But from this point the plays diverged.

In the one room the declarer saw nothing before him

but a rather commonplace affair, which he dealt with in routine fashion. Returning to his own hand with the King of Clubs, he led a Diamond, and when West put the Knave on the trick, finessed the Queen, which made. The declarer now cashed me, and West threw the King. Another Diamond was led, East taking the trick with the Ten and returning a Spade. South played the Nine, and West held up his Ace and put on the Ten, allowing dummy's King to take the trick. The thirteenth Diamond and the Heart Ace were cashed, but the declarer was one down, as he could not collect more than three Heart tricks, three Diamonds, one Spade, and one Club. He had realised too late that he could not get back to the closed hand to take the third Heart finesse.

The declarer in the other room made no such mistake. He analysed the hand carefully, and saw that ordinary finessing methods could not be followed for lack of clear entries in the closed hand. So at the third trick he cashed me before returning to the South hand with the King of Clubs. West dropped the Knave on the Diamond trick. but it did not help him. A Diamond was led from the South hand; West ducked; and dummy's Queen made. Another Diamond lead put West on play, as he had to take the trick with his King. He found nothing better to do than cash the Ace of Spades, intending to throw the lead to the table with another Spade. But dummy's King was thrown on the Ace, and now the Queen of Spades was an entry to the closed hand to enable the Heart finesse to be taken. So this declarer made four Heart tricks instead of three, and fulfilled his contract.

```
              ♠ K 8
              ♡ A Q 9 2
              ◇ A Q 5 3
              ♣ 10 6 4
♠ A 10 6              ♠ J 7 5 4 3 2
♡ K 10 8 7 4   N      ♡ 5
◇ K J 4      W   E    ◇ 10 9 8
♣ Q 5          S      ♣ A 9 8
              ♠ Q 9
              ♡ J 6 3
              ◇ 7 6 2
              ♣ K J 7 3 2
```

The cashing of me was the critical move in the campaign. It prevented East from taking a Diamond trick and making the fatal Spade lead which debarred South from using the Spade Queen as an entry. It doesn't matter whether West ducks the second round of Diamonds or puts up the King and throws dummy the lead with the Four of Diamonds. In the latter case the declarer simply throws the lead back to West with a Club. But what if West drops the King on me in the first round? The declarer would return to his hand with the King of Clubs as before, but would now take the Heart finesse at once, as, with the King out of the way, there would no longer be need to play Diamonds from the South hand. When the Heart finesse wins, the Queen of Diamonds would be played, West dropping the Knave. Another Diamond allows East to have the lead, but that is now harmless to the declarer, who cannot be hindered from making the King of Spades, the Ace of Hearts, and the thirteenth Diamond.

To round off my analysis I may add that East must always hold up his Ace when Clubs are first played. If he puts it on, he gives the declarer three extra tricks.

* * *

The Diamond Ace's exhaustive analysis must, I think,

have induced slight ennui among most of his audience, for their sounds of appreciation were polite rather than enthusiastic. That kindly creature, the Queen of Hearts, hastened to impart more warmth by remarking:

"To see right to the bottom of a situation most players would dismiss as quite undistinguished and take it to pieces like that is a sure sign of the master."

"Doubtless Your Majesty is right," returned the Three of Hearts. "But I was concerned in an adventure of freak distribution that also called for a master to handle. It was remarkable, too, for another reason, which I will not now disclose, as it would anticipate the whole point of the hand. Suffice it to say, then, that it was—"

A SAFETY PLAY EXTRAORDINARY

(*The Tale of the Three of Hearts*)

EVERYTHING ABOUT THIS HAND WAS EXTRAORDINARY—
the distribution, the bidding, the play. I shall let you see
only the North-South cards:

♠ K 4 3 2
♡ 2
◇ 8 5
♣ K J 10 6 4 2

```
        N
   W        E
        S
```

♠ A Q J 9 6
♡ A K Q 7 6 5 3
◇ A
♣ None

SOUTH	WEST	NORTH	EAST
2 ♡	3 ◇	No bid	5 ◇
5 ♡	Double	No bid	No bid
5 ♠	6 ◇	6 ♠	Double
Redouble	No bid	No bid	No bid

West led the King of Diamonds, which was taken by
South's Ace. The Ace of trumps was led, and West discarded
a Diamond. When he had first seen his partner's cards,
South had been inclined to feel that opponents' vigorous
bidding had jockeyed him into missing the Grand Slam.
Now he began to look carefully at the situation to see if his
actual contract was in danger.

He came to the conclusion that it was. For his double of

Hearts West must hold at least four to the Knave of that suit. Therefore, in order to set up the whole suit, a small Heart must be ruffed. That meant that East's trumps could not be drawn immediately—the ruff must first be taken. The obvious way to play was to cash the Ace of Hearts and then ruff a small Heart with dummy's King. But suppose West held all five opposing Hearts, and East was void of them? That was not at all unlikely on the bidding especially in view of West's double of Five Hearts. Again, what was more probable than that East's jump to Five Diamonds against an opening Forcing Two bid had been partly based on the distributional strength of a void? South himself was void of Clubs, and West had shown himself void of Spades. Why should not East be void of Hearts?

By this time the declarer was convinced that that almost certainly was the situation. If so, what could he do about it? The difficulty was not so much East's hypothetical lack of a Heart as West's hypothetical possession of five of the suit. For that would mean that two Hearts must be ruffed to establish the suit, and there was only one high trump in dummy to ruff with—East could overruff any of the others.

Suddenly, the declarer saw a way out—a safety play that would give up the 400 bonus for a redoubled over-trick if the Heart distribution was 4-1, but which would ensure the contract against defeat if the Heart distribution was indeed 5-0. He sacrificed me, his potential over-trick, by leading me at the third trick.

West played the Four, and with it took what must have been the cheapest trick ever made in the first round of a suit in a redoubled slam contract. But the declarer's bril-

♠ K 4 3 2
♡ 2
◇ 8 5
♣ K J 10 6 4 2

```
        N
   W         E
        S
```

♠ A Q J 9 6
♡ A K Q 7 6 5 3
◇ A
♣ None

liant precautionary play was justified, for East could not follow
to the Heart trick.

West returned a Diamond, but
in fact it made no difference
what he did. South trumped,
and led another small Heart for
dummy's King to ruff. A trump
was led through East, and the
finesse against East's Ten taken.
Trumps were now drawn, and
the established Heart suit and South's trumps made the
remainder of the tricks and the redoubled slam.

In the tale of the Ace of Diamonds and in many others
of the tales we have told you, Master Robert, there have
been spectacular sacrifices of high personages of the Pack.
But here I, a very lowly member of my tribe, was sacrificed
in circumstances where I had every reason for believing I
should make a trick in my own right. For surely the lowest card of a seven-card suit headed by the Ace-King-
Queen has good grounds for counting himself a winner.
That is why I said this was a remarkable hand—one of the
most remarkable I have ever come across. I was sacrificed
to West's Four in just the same way as a King is thrown
under an Ace. And I was potentially worth 400 points. But
my sacrifice made the declarer's contract safe.

*　　*　　*

The delight of the elfin throng, expressed with acute cries
and the clapping of tiny palms, was given words by that vi-
vacious little brunette, the Queen of Clubs.

286

"What could be more utterly satisfying to any lover of the game," she said, "than to size up a complex situation like that, think out the far-sighted and unusual play needed, and then triumphantly bring it off? Humans don't seem to have many pleasures that are quite unalloyed, but such an experience must be one of them."

"Quite true, Mam," interposed the Knave of Hearts, "but against that you must set the fact that there is only one way of playing a hand well, while bad play may create any number of beautiful variations. Sound analysis that correctly poses a problem and ingenuity that finds its sole solution may yield idealistic pleasure, but give me rather the wicked thrill of seizing and exploiting opportunities presented by opponents. To do the possible, however difficult, is one thing; but when there is bad play about, you may have the more robust and hot-blooded joy of doing the impossible— making contracts that are unmakeable and breaking contracts that are unbreakable."

"You're right, there, Jack," said the Ace of Clubs. "I once suffered extreme humiliation in a hand where the play was so amazingly bad that the whole affair became sheer entertainment. I have long since ceased to feel the affront I had to endure, and I think the story is worth relating for the comical number of mistakes made by the defence and for the clever impudence with which the declarer turned each one to his advantage, and proceeded to entice one or other opponent into further error. In the result, he did indeed achieve the impossible. From his point of view the defenders were a—"

BLEST PAIR OF BUNGLERS

(*The Tale of the Ace of Clubs*)

I WAS DEALT TO WEST, WHO WAS A POOR PLAYER, BUT didn't know it. In fact he rather fancied himself, and was for ever setting little traps and trying to avoid doing the obvious. His partner, East, was a poor player, and did know it. This made him timorous to a degree, so that he always imagined that the cards invisible to him lay against him and were positioned favourably for his opponents.

South and North were bright lads of an ultra-modern school of tortuous bidding which they acclaimed as scientific. Consequently they were inured to finding themselves at times in queer contracts. But up to a point they did know how to play their cards. Here are the deal and the bidding:

```
                    ♠ A K 4
                    ♡ 6 3
                    ♢ 9 6 5 3
                    ♣ Q 9 8 6
        ♠ 5                      ♠ Q 10 9 8 3
        ♡ K 9 8 7 2      N       ♡ 5
        ♢ 10 8 2     W       E   ♢ K 7 4
        ♣ A 5 4 2        S       ♣ K 10 7 3
                    ♠ J 7 6 2
                    ♡ A Q J 10 4
                    ♢ A Q J
                    ♣ J
```

South	West	North	East
1 ♠	No bid	2 ♠	No bid
3 ♡	No bid	3 ♠	No bid
4 ♠	No bid	No bid	Double
No bid	No bid	No bid	

North was perfectly aware that, on the system he and South were playing, he ought not to raise his partner's opening bid on fewer than four cards. However, with Ace-King of the suit, he decided to make this an exception, especially as the bid really did seem very fairly to express the nature and strength of his hand. When South saw dummy's cards, he maintained an unruffled composure. He knew his two opponents well, and despaired of no contract when they were defending.

East just managed to muster enough courage to double. His singleton Heart and North's denial of Hearts by merely returning to Spades gave East hope that West might hold something good in the suit. And anyway, he reassured himself, the double was a "free" double— by which, in company with so many other mediocre players, he quaintly meant that it was the double of a game bid. For one of his major phobias was terror lest he should double an opponent into game.

After considerable thought, West decided that his most cunning play would be to underlead me, and he chose the Deuce of Clubs. The declarer put on dummy's Eight, thereby suggesting to East that I was in the South hand. East meekly accepted the suggestion by playing the Ten, and South's bare Knave took the trick.

The declarer crossed to the table with the Ace of trumps, led a Heart, and finessed with the Knave. West craftily declined to take the trick. As South had bid Spades before Hearts, West decided that South had only four Hearts, and East a doubleton. West's plan was to take the second Heart finesse, and then lead a Heart for East to ruff. Smart play, that! he thought.

Again the declarer crossed to the table with a high trump, and learned the bad news of the Spade distribution as West discarded a small Club. Nothing daunted, the declarer led dummy's last Heart; and when East, anxiously hoarding

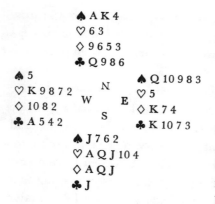

♠ A K 4
♡ 6 3
◇ 9 6 5 3
♣ Q 9 8 6

♠ 5
♡ K 9 8 7 2
◇ 10 8 2
♣ A 5 4 2

N
W E
S

♠ Q 10 9 8 3
♡ 5
◇ K 7 4
♣ K 10 7 3

♠ J 7 6 2
♡ A Q J 10 4
◇ A Q J
♣ J

up his trumps, threw a small Club, South took the trick with his Ace.

I saw a slight smile hovering on South's lips, and guessed he was saying to himself:

"What ghastly distribution! But these two fellows are the most heavenly pair of blunderers ever sent in answer to a declarer's prayer. They just don't want to make tricks. Let's see if I can go on giving them a design for bungling."

He now led the Ten of Hearts. West played low; dummy threw a Diamond; and East trumped with the Nine. What was East to lead now? If he led the Queen of trumps, it would set up South's Knave. He still feared South held me, and was just waiting for him to play into the Ace-Queen tenace. So East led a small Diamond, South finessed with the Queen, and led the Queen of Hearts. West covered with the King; dummy ruffed; and East overruffed. Now East cashed his Queen of trumps, and, with the obsession about me still deterring him from a Club lead, returned another Diamond.

South finessed with the Knave; cashed the Ace of Diamonds; and led his last trump, the Knave. West had two cards left—me and the Nine of Hearts. He stared at us. He had lost count of the Hearts. Weren't they all out by now?

There had been several rounds of them, and only one round of Clubs. Surely South's last card must be a Club. Anyway, West felt he just couldn't part from me, his one and only Ace. So he threw the Nine of Hearts, and South's Four of Hearts made the last trick and the contract. All the declarer had lost was three trump tricks.

It was rather terrible for me at the time to find I was falling uselessly on that thirteenth round; but I soon forgot my woe in listening to the post-mortem between West and East. While West was dealing the next hand, they explained to each other carefully why they had played as they did.

East kept on saying he was convinced throughout that I was in the South hand. West reiterated that he had hoped to give East a third-round ruff in Hearts, and that there had been only one round of Clubs. And so on and so on. South merely held that ghost of a smile on his lips.

* * *

The Club Ace won a meed of laughter, and the King of Diamonds remarked:

"Yes, bad play has its charm. It introduces an element of the unpredictable, the fortuitous into the most prosaic of deals. That is why the game has so wide an appeal, why it is enjoyed by players of all degrees of skill. Like golf, bridge fascinates the poorest player equally with the top-ranking expert."

"Well, I think it's very fortunate that bad play doesn't spoil the game," put in the Knave of Clubs, "for it is undeniable that there is more bad play than good at the card table. I think you will confess, Master Robert, that you bridge writers give a false picture of the game by your articles and books dealing with striking situations and brilliant attack and defence. We People of the Pack have all too much reason to know that mistakes are a recurrent factor in the game as it is really played, and that the general run of hands are straightforward and dull. What can make these multitudinous ordinary hands interesting is the very fact that players may and do go wrong over them, and then all kinds of piquant opportunities occur—to be seized or neglected, exploited or muddled, according to the calibre of the players concerned. We have given you a fair leavening of such hands, Master Robert; and I wonder if your public will relish them, or whether they will find too many examples of human frailty in your book."

With the Wee Folk anxiously hanging on my answer, I smilingly told them it would be their responsibility if the public did think that. All I was going to do was faithfully to retell their tales.

"It's going to be your book," I assured them, "not mine."

They seemed highly pleased.

"I think the public like realism," said the Nine of Spades, "as long as it is presented romantically. And if that is a paradox, I can't help it. The story I wish to relate is realistic enough, for it centres on the simple physiological fact that it is possible for a bridge player to feel sleepy. Where the romance comes in is in the resourcefulness of the declarer, who took full advantage of—"

A SOMNAMBULISTIC DEFENCE

(The Tale of the Nine of Spades)

A BUSY DAY, A GOOD DINNER, AN EVENING OF BRIDGE AT THE club, now ending with the final rubber, which had already lasted, as final rubbers do, an unconscionable time, had created in East a longing for his bed. South, quite wide awake, had not failed to notice his opponent's drooping eyelids, and had heard him say to the steward, who asked him what he had had: "Four Spades to the Ace, five Hearts to—I mean, I've had a black coffee and two whiskeys."

However, the rubber would soon be over now, East consoled himself, for he and West had a part-score of 80 in the third game. With an effort, East jerked himself awake, and dealt these hands:

```
                  ♠ Q J 6 5 4 2
                  ♡ None
                  ◇ J 8 6 4
                  ♣ 9 7 3
    ♠ None              N         ♠ K 10 8
    ♡ A J 9 8 6                   ♡ K 10 7 5 4 3
    ◇ A K 2      W        E       ◇ 10 7
    ♣ Q J 10 8 4        S         ♣ K 6
                  ♠ A 9 7 3
                  ♡ Q 2
                  ◇ Q 9 5 3
                  ♣ A 5 2
```

EAST	SOUTH	WEST	NORTH
No bid	No bid	1 ♣	No bid
No bid	1 ♠	2 ♠	No bid
3 ♡	No bid	No bid	3 ♠
Double	No bid	4 ♡	4 ♠
Double	No bid	No bid	No bid

During the bidding East had manfully concentrated his attention on his cards. Now, while his partner was considering what to lead, he felt somnolence descending upon him once more. West started off with the Queen of Clubs, and now South was inspecting dummy's hand. Drowsily East noted with satisfaction that the opening lead made his King good, but it did not occur to him that he ought to over-take his partner's Queen.

South's Ace took the trick, and that astute individual decided to try to exploit East's lack of awareness. If West's bid of Two Spades was correct, it meant that East held all three outstanding Spades. So, playing quickly and confidently, he crossed to the table, and at once led the Deuce of trumps. As he had hoped might happen, East lethargically played the Eight; and South took the trick with me. Thus East's Spade stopper had vanished, as both his trumps could be picked up by the declarer at any time. If East had played the Ten, it would have driven out South's Ace, and East must make the King, and, in addition, would still have had the Eight of trumps in hand with which to ruff a Diamond.

Returning to dummy with another Heart ruff, the declarer led the Queen of trumps; East covered with the King; and South's Ace took the trick. South now led a small Diamond. Dangerous play, this, but if he had first drawn East's last trump with dummy's Knave, he would then have had to lead Diamonds from the table. West would have taken the trick, and led a Club to East's King, and East could then have got rid of the lead with his last Diamond, and the defence must make another Club. The declarer's only chance was to lead a Diamond from his own hand in the hope that West would play low.

That is just what West did, and dummy's Knave made. Now the declarer drew East's last trump, and led a small

```
                ♠ Q J 6 5 4 2
                ♡ None
                ◇ J 8 6 4
                ♣ 9 7 3
♠ None                      ♠ K 10 8
♡ A J 9 8 6      N          ♡ K 10 7 5 4 3
◇ A K 2       W     E       ◇ 10 7
♣ Q J 10 8 4     S          ♣ K 6
                ♠ A 9 7 3
                ♡ Q 2
                ◇ Q 9 5 3
                ♣ A 5 2
```

Diamond from dummy to West's King. West returned a Club, and East's King made. East had only Hearts left, and had to lead one. South ruffed, discarding dummy's last Club, and led a Diamond. West's Ace made, but the defence could take no other trick, as the declarer's Diamond was established. The contract was thus made, with the loss of two Diamonds and a Club.

West said to East:

"Do you realise that the contract should have been defeated by three tricks, and that we have a Small Slam in either Clubs or Hearts? Really, my dear fellow, I think you'd find it cheaper to sleep at the Ritz than here at the bridge table."

"I daresay I should," replied East, amiably. "But you know you weren't so wonderfully wide-eyed yourself, or you would have jumped in with the King of Diamonds on the first round. I think I should have been awake enough then to signal with the Ten, and you could have cashed your Ace and given me a Diamond ruff."

* * *

This tale was received rather coldly, and the Queen of Hearts, wrinkling her nose distastefully, said:

"Not a very nice man, South, I think. He can't, I suppose,

be exactly accused of unfairness in deliberately trying to profit by an opponent's tiredness, but it's not the sort of exploit to congratulate oneself about."

"Perhaps not," said the King of Diamonds, "but the real moral of that story is the importance of physical fitness. An American critic once said that bridge was 90 per cent. concentration. A transatlantic exaggeration, may be, but concentration is indeed a *sine qua non* of good play; and concentration in its turn, depends on physical endurance. That is why championship bridge, with its long-drawn contests and its hectic atmosphere, is for the relatively young. The old and those in the shady half of middle age can enjoy and do well at rubber bridge or short minor duplicate matches, but for Big Bridge stamina is every bit as essential as it is for Big Golf or Wimbledon lawn tennis."

"I note you were careful to say 'the relatively young,' " remarked the precisely-minded Knave of Spades. "The very young lack the experience that is quite as essential to good play as is stamina. It is rare to find a front-rank player who is less than thirty. I should say the best years of a bridge player's life are from thirty to forty-five. Before that, he lacks judgment, and after that, he tires too quickly. Though, of course, you will find exceptions."

"But whatever his age," put in the Seven of Clubs, "the greatest gift a player can have is to make his mistakes— and they all make 'em, expert and novice alike, only different ones—at the right moment. You have all been talking as if mistakes were invariably sheer dynamite to their perpetrators, forgetting that at bridge a mistake can pay dividends as high as those that come from the most brilliant coup of

a master. You remember the case of Marmaduke Haddle.
I once had an adventure that illustrates vividly how profitable a thing a blunder can be. It took a tipsy man to make
it and his sober partner to turn it to account. So I think—
if you will forgive the dog-Latin—we may call it—"

EX VINO DUPLICITAS

(*The Tale of the Seven of Clubs*)

BRIDGE PLAYERS ARE THE MOST ABSTEMIOUS OF FOLK.
Many don't drink at all while at the card-table, and it is
seldom anyone has more than one or two drinks during the
evening. But with a player who is young, and who has come

straight from a wedding where the best champagne flowed freely, it may be different. Anyway, it was so with the North of my story, who had just been best man to his closest chum, and had now dropped into the club for a rubber or two before dinner. He carried it off all right, mind you. He was just pleasantly and harmlessly muzzy, when, after only once misdealing, he managed quite well to distribute the cards **thus**:

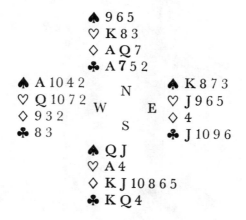

♠ 9 6 5
♡ K 8 3
◇ A Q 7
♣ A 7 5 2

♠ A 10 4 2
♡ Q 10 7 2
◇ 9 3 2
♣ 8 3

♠ K 8 7 3
♡ J 9 6 5
◇ 4
♣ J 10 9 6

♠ Q J
♡ A 4
◇ K J 10 8 6 5
♣ K Q 4

That was how North dealt, but in sorting his own hand he took me for a Spade, and placed me among the cards of that suit, thus imagining he held Nine-Seven-Six-Five of Spades. I listened in, and heard him muttering to himself:

"Count of 13. Gotter open with something. Spades no dam' good—only four to the measly Nine. Better bid a 'prepared Club.' That way can s'pport anything bloke across the way says. Better for him to play the hand. Discretion better part of thingummy, here."

So he bid One Club. South responded with One Diamond, which North hastily raised to Two Diamonds. South now tried Two Spades. Repeating to himself: "Must s'pport anything bloke across way says, and have got four Spades for him," North raised Two Spades to Three Spades.

He blinked when South now jumped to Six Diamonds, but consoled himself with:

"This is bloke's funeral. He's gotter play the darned thing."

West led the Eight of Clubs, and North tabled his hand, remarking defensively:

"Got what I said. Good Diamond s'pport and four Spades to an abs'lutely t'riffic Nine."

"You have nothing of the sort," replied South, with a grin. "Look what nuptial bubbly's done to you—made you put the Club Seven among your Spades. Oh, well, I might as well play it now as any time."

He leaned across, picked me out of the Spade suit, and threw me on the trick. East played the Six of Clubs, and South's King made.

The declarer, though naturally disappointed at not finding the Ace or King of Spades with his partner, was gratified that he had succeeded in inhibiting a Spade lead. What now? The lead of the Club Eight and East's play of the Six made it unlikely that the suit would break evenly and provide a parking place for one of South's Spades on dummy's fourth Club. He decided to bank on the Ace-King of Spades being split, and on opponents' continuing to be deceived about the suit.

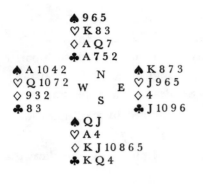

♠ 9 6 5
♡ K 8 3
◇ A Q 7
♣ A 7 5 2

♠ A 10 4 2
♡ Q 10 7 2
◇ 9 3 2
♣ 8 3

♠ K 8 7 3
♡ J 9 6 5
◇ 4
♣ J 10 9 6

♠ Q J
♡ A 4
◇ K J 10 8 6 5
♣ K Q 4

Crossing to the table with the Ace of trumps, he calmly led the Five of Spades, and when East played low, put on the Knave from his own hand. West took the trick with the Ace, and after some thought, led a trump, with the intention of trying to prevent South from ruffing his fourth Spade in dummy—for he not unnaturally placed South with four of the suit.

The declarer took the trick; cashed the Ace and King of Hearts; and then reeled off all his trumps. East was squeezed. He must either give up the King of Spades or unguard his Knave of Clubs. Reckless though it seemed, South's play of Spades at the third trick was a necessity. A trick must be lost in order to bring about a squeeze position, and as that trick had to be in Spades, the suit must be played at once before either partner could signal to the other his possession of a high card in it.

In the end-play, East unguarded his Clubs, and kept the King of Spades, so the last three tricks were made by South's Club Queen and dummy's Ace and Five of the suit. Whereupon North remarked happily:

"Lucky after all I had four Clubs instead of four Spades, what?"

"A neat piece of deception play," approved the Ace of Spades.

"Yes," assented the Four of Hearts, "but made easier of accomplishment by the fact that the declarer had bid Spades. These bluff plays were where a player pretends to be strong in a weak suit or weak in a strong suit, are easy enough to do, but they require nerve. They have to be executed in a perfectly natural manner. If a player tries to bring one off while feeling all the time as frightened as a rabbit, I've noticed time and again that it just doesn't work. Now I once had an adventure in which a declarer similarly had two immediate losers in a suit, and yet, without any bogus bidding to help him, he managed by the unblushing hardihood with which he performed his piece of trickery, to steer the defence away from it. This he did, not by seeking directly to inhibit the play of the suit, but by persuading the defence to play another suit. It was a case of—"

CAMOUFLAGE BY DISCARD

(*The Tale of the Four of Hearts*)

I WAS DEALT TO A SEASONED AND COOL-HEADED SOUTH, AND
there was a certain liveliness about the bidding.

```
            ♠ K
            ♡ K J 3
            ◊ Q J 9 5 3
            ♣ J 10 4 2

               N
        W            E
               S

            ♠ A J 10 9 6 5 2
            ♡ A Q 4
            ◊ 8 4
            ♣ 9
```

East	South	West	North
1 ♣	2 ♠	No bid	3 ◊
No bid	3 ♠	No bid	3 N-T
Double	4 ♠	Double	No bid
No bid	No bid		

West led the Five of Clubs. East won with the King, and returned the Club Ace, which South ruffed, West playing the Club Seven. South led a small trump to dummy's King, and at once played out dummy's Knave of Clubs. When East followed suit, South unhesitatingly threw me on the trick. In making this queer discard South argued thus:

"I have lost a Club trick, and on West's double I'm doomed to lose a trump trick to the Queen of Spades. And I have two losing Diamonds. There would be no point in ruffing the Club Knave, as it's obvious West has led from four to the Queen and she wouldn't drop. I could discard a diamond loser, but then I should still be one down, losing two Clubs, a trump, and a Diamond. Now it is practically certain from East's double of Three No-Trumps that West cannot have the Ace of Diamonds. In that case he has no means of knowing, if I let him win this Club trick, whether to return a Diamond or a Heart. That gives me a chance to lead him astray and induce him to think my losing tricks are in Hearts instead of in Diamonds. So I'll discard my Four of Hearts."

West took the trick with the Queen of Clubs, and what could he think but that South had executed the familiar manoeuvre of throwing a loser on a loser, and was planning to rid himself of another Heart loser on the established Ten of Clubs? So West returned a Heart, and South proceeded to make his contract.

Taking the trick with the Ace of Hearts, he cashed the Ace of trumps, both opponents following suit. He then crossed to the table by overtaking the Queen of Hearts with the King, and discarded a Diamond from his hand on dummy's Knave of Hearts. Dummy's Ten of Clubs was cashed, and South's last Diamond discarded on it. All the defence could now make was West's Queen of trumps. So South lost only two Clubs and a trump trick.

A piquant feature of the play was that if West had suspected the trick that was being played on him, and had returned a Diamond when he got the lead with the Queen of Clubs, South would have lost five tricks—two Clubs, two Diamonds, and a trump. The declarer risked being down an extra trick in order to set the trap for West.

*   *   *

"I really feel rather sorry for all these poor duped defenders," said the Queen of Hearts. "It is so seldom the other way about. I am beginning to think the declarer has too big an advantage. It makes good defence too difficult, and declarers get away with too many bad contracts."

"I can't agree with you there, Your Majesty," put in the Ten of Hearts. "Think of the number of perfectly good contracts that are defeated by unforeseeable duplications of values or by fantastically unlucky opposing distribution. I remember one occasion on which the declarer of a Small Slam, with all the Aces and Kings, two Queens, and a six-card suit, ran into two 5-0 splits of opposing cards. Only the most expert adroitness, that realised I was the key to the situation, saved the day. It all happened in rather curious circumstances, which I can best describe as arising out of—"

AN EXPECTANT FATHER'S LEGACY
(*The Tale of the Ten of Hearts*)

THE PLAYER I WAS DEALT TO WAS A SOMEWHAT NONDE-
script young man who seldom came to the club except at
weekends. But this was a Wednesday, and he had arrived
about three o'clock and had been playing in a singularly
nervous and absent-minded fashion for a couple of hours.

He was only moderately good at the game, so it passed unnoticed that he had been making rather more mistakes than usual. He was sitting South, with the score love-all in the third game, when North dealt these hands:

```
                    ♠ A K
                    ♡ A K Q 7
                    ◇ J
                    ♣ A K Q 6 5 3
    ♠ J 6 5 4 3         N         ♠ Q 8
    ♡ None                        ♡ J 9 5 4 3
    ◇ Q 9 3      W         E      ◇ 8 7 6 5 4 2
    ♣ J 10 9 8 7        S         ♣ None
                    ♠ 10 9 7 2
                    ♡ 10 8 6 2
                    ◇ A K 10
                    ♣ 4 2
```

Playing the Forcing Two, North opened with Two Clubs, and South responded with Three No-Trumps, which North raised to Six No-Trumps. West doubled, and North promptly redoubled.

West led the Knave of Clubs, and when dummy's Queen was put on, East discarded a small Diamond. I felt South register dismay, as well he might, for now the Club suit could not be used as the main basis for fulfilling the contract. So he tried out the Heart suit, leading the Ace. This time West showed out, discarding a small Spade.

The second blow quite disconcerted South. I sensed his distracted thought:

"All I can make are three Hearts, three Club, two Spades, and two Diamonds—ten tricks. Where on earth are the other two to come from? Perhaps, with all this awful distribution, someone has the Queen-Knave of Spades bare. It seems the only hope."

So he played out the Ace and King of Spades, but only the Queen dropped. I heard him mutter:

"Clearly West has the Knave of Spades. So I could set up a Spade trick by returning to my hand with the Ace of Diamonds and leading the Ten of Spades. But then there is no entry back to my hand for me to cash the Spade Nine. Oh, dear, this is terrible. I don't know what to try for now. I suppose I had better just go down quietly."

It was at this moment that a steward came into the room to tell South he was wanted on the telephone. The young man sprang to his feet, threw his cards on the table, and rushed from the room without a word to anyone.

"What extraordinary behaviour!" exclaimed East. "Surely he could have played out the hand. Fancy just dashing off like that!"

"It's easily explained," said North. "His wife's having a baby to-day. It's their first, too. He told me about it when he arrived this afternoon. He made such a nuisance of himself at home that the doctor and nurse sent him off to play bridge, promising to ring him up here as soon as there was any news. He's been like a cat on hot bricks all afternoon."

Just then the steward returned, with a broad grin on his face and the information that South would not be coming back to finish the rubber.

"He went to the telephone," said the steward; "listened a moment; exclaimed: 'Good Lord! You don't say so!' beamed all over, and ran out of the club just as he was, shouting Taxi! Taxi!"

"I wonder what that means," said North.

Dr. McGuire, who was sitting in a near-by armchair, reading the evening paper, chuckled.

"With an expectant father, you never can tell," he declared. "It might be quads; or just that he wanted a boy or a girl and has got it; or just that herself and the babe are both fine."

"Well, that's all right then," said West. "But what about this hand? North had the cheek to redouble, don't forget; and I want my pound of flesh."

"I can't play it," said North. "I've been looking over the other hands. Perhaps Dr. McGuire would be good enough to take it on."

"Yes, come on, Doc," agreed the two defenders. And West added: "It'll be interesting to see how low you can keep the penalty."

So they told the Doctor the bidding, and showed him the first four tricks. The situation when he took it over was:

```
                ♠ None
                ♡ K Q 7
                ◇ J
                ♣ K Q 6 5 3
   ♠ J 6                      ♠ None
   ♡ None     N              ♡ J 9 5 4
   ◇ Q 9 3  W     E          ◇ 8 7 6 5 4
   ♣ 10 9 8 7   S            ♣ None
                ♠ 10 9
                ♡ 10 8 6
                ◇ A K 10
                ♣ 4
```

313

Remarking, "Let's see what blessed sort of legacy the expectant father has left me," Dr. McGuire pondered deeply a few moments. Then he turned to West.

"Was it a small penalty ye were daring me to get it down to?" the old Irishman asked. "Well, if I cash the King and Queen of Hearts and Clubs, and then throw you in with a Club, you've got to lead away from your Queen of Diamonds. But first, of course, you'd put me one down by making your Jack of Spades. Still, that does away with your dream of a thousand points for two down redoubled, doesn't it? But I think I can do even better than that, if I pay less attention to you for the moment, and see what I can get out of the fine broth of a boy on me right."

So saying the old man, who was plainly enjoying himself, cashed dummy's King of Hearts, and then led the Seven of the suit. East took the trick with his Knave, and returned a Diamond, South's Ace making. At this point Dr. McGuire cashed the King of Diamonds, and with a positive leer of pleasure at his own ingenuity, discarded on it dummy's Queen of Hearts. This brilliant move made me the master card of the suit, and kept the lead in the South hand. The Doctor led me, saying as he did so to West:

"It's your turn, Mr. Pound-of-Flesh. What are ye going to give on this card?"

West, who had thrown his small Spade on the King of Hearts and a Club on the trick East won with his Heart Knave, was subjected to a triple squeeze. It did not matter what he did. If he threw his Spade Knave, South's two Spades were good; and if he threw a Club, dummy's Clubs were all masters. So he gave up the Queen of Diamonds.

314

Dr. McGuire at once led the Ten of Diamonds, and West was squeezed again. Thus the redoubled contract was made.

*   *   *

When the special applause the Little Folk seemed to reserve for squeeze-play had died down, the Knave of Hearts remarked:

"Dr. McGuire's handling of the situation is a striking illustration of the uses to which the principle of promotion can be put. When the Seven of Hearts was led, the very existence of the Ten in the South hand compelled East to put up his Knave. That promoted the Ten to equality with the Queen, so that all that remained to keep the lead away from dummy, which would have been forced fatally to lead Clubs, was to discard the Queen, making the Ten the master card and an inescapable squeeze card against West. I take off my hat to that subtile old Irish doctor."

"So do I," said the Six of Diamonds. "There is something peculiarly attractive about a triple squeeze, and I am going to give yet another example. But of a different kind—something really intricate and abounding in pleasing variations. I am doing so because I think you will agree, Master Robert, that your book—our book—ought to contain one classic specimen of the true—"

DOUBLE DUMMY PROBLEM

(Analysed by the Six of Diamonds)

INSTEAD OF MY TELLING A TALE, MASTER ROBERT, I SUGGEST
you place before your readers this problem. Its type is in
my opinion the best of all double dummy problems because

it is the most comprehensive. All fifty-two cards are involved, and the declarer, South, must make his contract—here Seven No-Trumps—against any opening lead and any defence.

```
                    ♠ A K J 3
                    ♡ J 3 2
                    ◇ J 4 2
                    ♣ A 3 2
    ♠ Q 9 8 6 5 4          N          ♠ 7
    ♡ None                            ♡ 10 9 8 7 6
    ◇ 10 9 8 7        W        E      ◇ Q 5 3
    ♣ Q J 10                S         ♣ 9 8 7 6
                    ♠ 10 2
                    ♡ A K Q 5 4
                    ◇ A K 6
                    ♣ K 5 4
```

Let us first count the certain winners in the North-South hands. There are four Heart tricks, three Spades, two Diamonds, and two Clubs—eleven tricks in all. Two more tricks must be developed, and a glance at the cards shows that they cannot be gained by running off any suit, as all four suits are guarded in the opponents' hands. It is clear that the situation calls for squeeze-play.

A second glance at the hands reveals that if West makes the opening lead of a Spade, he gives away a trick at once—four Spade tricks can now be made. The remaining missing trick can then be readily acquired by a simple squeeze. For example, all the declarer need do is to take his four Spade tricks and cash the Ace and King of Clubs, and East is squeezed at the sixth trick in the two red suits.

But if West starts with a Diamond or a Club, he gives away nothing, and now no simple squeeze, yielding only one extra trick, will serve. The triple squeeze must be brought into play. In a triple squeeze a player is squeezed in three suits, and has to give up a trick by discarding from one of the three suits. He is then subsequently squeezed again in the remaining two suits, and compelled to surrender the other lacking trick. The Ten of Hearts in his tale told of a triple squeeze, but it involved throw-in play. In a Grand Slam the declarer is denied that aid. Our task here is thus simpler in form and harder in practice. Let us, then, examine how the forces against us in the defenders' hands are balanced.

West has the Spades stopped and East the Hearts. Each defender controls the Club suit independently of the other, but their protection of Diamonds is held jointly between them. East has the highest opposing Diamond, the Queen. The declarer can at will, however, transfer the protection of the Diamond suit to West by leading the Knave from dummy. East must cover, and then West alone will have the Diamonds stopped.

If West opens with a Diamond or a Club, the declarer's course of action will be founded on the same principles. The play may be divided into two parts—the prelude and the end-play. In the prelude we cash the high cards of one major suit, and the defender holding the other major suit must relinquish his protection of one or other of the three suits he holds. If he gives up his protection of Diamonds or of his major suit, he surrenders a trick at once, and creates a relatively easy situation for the declarer; and if he parts from his

```
              ♠ A K J 3
              ♡ J 3 2
              ◇ J 4 2
              ♣ A 3 2
♠ Q 9 8 6 5 4       N        ♠ 7
♡ None          W       E    ♡ 10 9 8 7 6
◇ 10 9 8 7          S        ◇ Q 5 3
♣ Q J 10                     ♣ 9 8 7 6
              ♠ 10 2
              ♡ A K Q 5 4
              ◇ A K 6
              ♣ K 5 4
```

Club stopper, he passes the protection of the suit over to his partner, who will then have three suits to protect—his major suit, Diamonds, and Clubs. Overburdened with duties, this hand can then be squeezed by the cashing of the high cards in the second major suit. In short, the prelude must be directed against one defender and the end-play against the other. And now let us put these principles into effect.

West leads the Ten of Diamonds. We must at once decide against whom to direct the end-play. If against West, we must transfer the Diamond holding to him by playing the Knave from dummy. But this would not suffice because the three Spade tricks we can make now would not force East in the prelude to make a fatal discard, which would be indispensable. Therefore, we decide to steer the end-play against East and the prelude against West. The play goes:

Trick One, small Diamond from dummy, small Diamond from East, South's Ace takes; Trick Two, Heart Knave; Trick Three, Heart King; Trick Four, Heart Ace; Trick Five, Heart Queen, West discarding a Club and North a Spade.

These five tricks constitute the prelude, by which West has been forced to abandon his Club stopper. Now comes the end-play against East:

Trick Six, Spade finesse; Trick Seven, Spade King; Trick Eight, Spade Ace.

East is squeezed in three suits. Whatever he discards, he surrenders a trick, and the subsequent cashing of this trick by the declarer will squeeze him again, and compel him to yield up the second missing trick. For example, if East discards a Diamond to Trick Eight, South also discards a Diamond—me—and the play continues thus:

Trick Nine, King of Diamonds, dropping East's Queen; Trick Ten, declarer crosses to the table with the Ace of Clubs; Trick Eleven, Knave of Diamonds (the trick given up by East in the first squeeze), and East is squeezed again in Clubs and Hearts.

And now let us suppose West leads the Queen of Clubs. South's King must take this trick, for South has entries in Diamonds and North's Club Ace must be reserved as entry to dummy for the end-play. In the previous variation Club entries in both hands were a necessity. Now the lead has robbed us of a Club entry. So the end-play cannot be directed against East. This time the prelude is designed to force East to give up his Club stopper and to transfer the Diamond protection, too, to West, against whom the end-play will be steered. The prelude goes:

Trick One, Club King; Trick Two, Spade finesse; Trick Three, Spade Ace; Trick Four, Spade King; Trick Five, Diamond Knave, covered by East's Queen, South's King winning.

Then comes the end-play:

Trick Six, Heart Knave; Trick Seven, Heart Queen; Trick Eight, Heart King; Trick Nine, Heart Ace.

West is squeezed in three suits, just as East was before.

These are the two chief variations. I think you should leave it to your readers, Master Robert, to work out the minor variations that occur when one or other defender, pressed in the prelude, gives up control of a suit other than Clubs. Many different kinds of simple and bilateral squeezes crop up in these variations.

But in its two main variations the composition of this problem is something of a technical record, for it is a bilateral triple squeeze—that is, a triple squeeze that operates against both defenders. In the prelude the one is squeezed, and in the end-play the other.

I confess that my great liking for this problem is because the whole play depends on the handling of the Diamond suit; and I am the most important card in that suit, since I bring about the downfall of West in the most difficult variation, when the opening lead robs the declarer of one of his two Club entries.

*　*　*

To my astonishment the intricate multiformity of the Diamond Six's problem drew sounds of only moderate appreciation. Were the Wee Folk actually beginning to be surfeited with squeezes? Then I noticed that all the rest of the Diamonds were bunched together to one side, with the little Four—the only citizen of the Pack who had still to tell his tale—in their midst. The other three tribes watched, with worried faces, from a short distance. In a moment or two the Queen stepped out of the Diamond group, and came towards me.

"Our Four is quite willing to tell you the fifty-second tale,

Master Robert," she said; "but he's shy and embarrassed about it because the only outstanding hand he can really recollect is one you yourself played."

"Well, why should that matter?" I asked. "Hasn't his brother, the Diamond Five, already recalled a sad failure of mine?"

"We reminded him of that," explained the Queen, with one of her dazzling smiles; "but he says you had forgotten that hand, while the hand he wants to relate you played with such mastery, and it turned on so unusual a situation, that you are sure to remember it well. And what's the use he wants to know, of his repeating back to you an exploit of your own which you can't possibly have forgotten?"

"Every use," I replied firmly. "It's he who has forgotten something—our book. What better could I ask than that one of you should counterbalance the Diamond Five's pillorying of me with another hand in which my play is made to shine, and which I myself could not recall without being accused of blowing my own trumpet? Why, he'd be doing me a very great service, for which I thank him gratefully in advance."

On hearing this, the Diamond Four came forward, beaming happily, and said:

"It was a good hand, Master Robert, a fiendishly difficult hand. You had to have luck on your side as well as skill. In the end you made up your contract by an ingenious coup unknown to me, and for which, I am sure, no name exists. I suggest that your discovery of this novel playing device deserves that it should bear your name. So I shall call my story—"

THE ROBERT COUP

(The Tale of the Four of Diamonds)

I HAD NO GLORIOUS PART TO PLAY. INDEED, IT WAS A SELF-effacing role you assigned to me, Master Robert. But I was glad to be dealt to you, and I took pleasure in reading your mind and watching how it grappled with the thorny difficulties that lay in the way of your making the contract.

With East-West only vulnerable, you dealt these cards, sitting South:

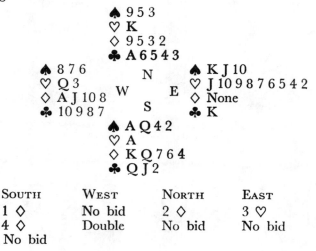

	♠ 9 5 3	
	♡ K	
	◇ 9 5 3 2	
	♣ A 6 5 4 3	

♠ 8 7 6		♠ K J 10
♡ Q 3		♡ J 10 9 8 7 6 5 4 2
◇ A J 10 8		◇ None
♣ 10 9 8 7		♣ K

	♠ A Q 4 2
	♡ A
	◇ K Q 7 6 4
	♣ Q J 2

SOUTH	WEST	NORTH	EAST
1 ◇	No bid	2 ◇	3 ♡
4 ◇	Double	No bid	No bid
No bid			

West led the Queen of Hearts to your Ace. You led the King of trumps; West took the trick with his Ace; and you learned, not unexpectedly, the bad news about trumps when East discarded a Heart. West returned the Ten of Clubs, and you said to yourself:

"Not a very hopeful outlook. I have lost one trick already. I may have to lose two more Diamonds, a Club, and at least one Spade. Two down. What does the lead of the Club Ten mean? West's a good lawyer, and I don't believe he'd lead the Ten from the once-guarded King. Anyway, if that's his holding, I can't make the contract at all. It's much more likely that East has the King, in which case I'm sunk again unless it happens to be bare. And why shouldn't it be? Obviously, the deal is freakish. East must have a whale of a lot of Hearts to jump to Three when he is vulnerable. I had the singleton Ace of Hearts and dummy the singleton King. If there's anything in this Law of Symmetry idea, it wouldn't be surprising that East should have a high singleton, too. Anyhow, I've not really much choice."

So you put up dummy's Ace of Clubs, Master Robert, and dropped East's King. That heartened you a bit, and you now led a small Spade from dummy, and successfully finessed the Queen. I heard you tell yourself:

"This contract isn't lost yet. After those two pieces of good fortune, I can make it if I can find a way of losing only one more trump."

You cashed the Ace of Spades and the Queen and Knave of Clubs, East discarding Hearts. Now you led the Deuce of Spades, and East got the lead with his King, and played back a Heart. You paused to consider.

"I have a complete count on the hands. West has the Nine of Clubs left and Knave-Ten-Eight of trumps, and as there have been three full rounds of Spades, his fifth card must be a Heart. East has nothing but Hearts. So the situation is:

```
                ♠ None
                ♡ None
                ◇ 9 5 3
                ♣ 6 5
   ♠ None          N          ♠ None
   ♡ x                        ♡ x x x x x
   ◇ J 10 8    W       E      ◇ None
   ♣ 9            S           ♣ None
                ♠ 4
                ♡ None
                ◇ Q J 6 4
                ♣ None
```

```
              ♠ 9 5 3
              ♡ K
              ♦ 9 5 3 2
              ♣ A 6 5 4 3
♠ 8 7 6              ♠ K J 10
♡ Q 3        S      ♡ J 10 9 8 7 6 5 4 2
♦ A J 10 8  W   E   ♦ None
♣ 10 9 8 7   S      ♣ K
              ♠ A Q 4 2
              ♡ A
              ♦ K Q 7 6 4
              ♣ Q J 2
```

"Is there any way of playing so as to lose only one more trick? If I ruff East's Heart lead in my hand, and lead a Spade, West would ruff with the Ten of Diamonds and return a Club, and then he must make another trump trick. That's no good. Well, suppose I discard the Spade from my hand on East's Heart lead, and ruff in dummy. Then I could ruff a Club in my hand, and lead a small trump. West would take with the Ten, and then he would lead the Knave of trumps, dropping dummy's Nine. My Queen of Diamonds would take the trick, but then I must play my trump Seven for him to take the trick with his trump Eight. That's no good either. But it has given me an idea. It's clear now that the only position in which I could lose only one more trick would be if I could reduce West's hand to three trumps and no other cards, and could then lead the Spade from my hand. West would have to trump, but dummy needn't—that's the whole point—and so I wouldn't have to bare the Nine in dummy for West's Knave to drop it. Can I bring about that position?"

And then, Master Robert, you saw how it could be done, and the Robert Coup was born. You ruffed East's Heart lead with me in your hand, and then overruffed in dummy with that graceless brother of mine, the Five. A Club was led from dummy, and ruffed in the closed hand, and you

326

had brought about the position you desired. You led your Spade; West ruffed with the Ten; and you discarded dummy's last Club. West now had to lead from his Knave-Eight of trumps to the Nine-Three in dummy and the Queen-Seven in your hand, and so you made the last two tricks and your contract, having lost only a Spade and two trumps.

You ruffed with me, not to take the trick with me, but to get rid of me—to shorten your trump-holding. By overtaking the trick in dummy you virtually discarded me on the Five of Trumps. To discard a trump on another trump of your own—that is something new. I name it the Robert Coup.

*　　*　　*

The Little People applauded and cheered long and vigorously, and I had to fall in with their kindly intent by bowing my acknowledgments again and again, like any star of the stage; though I confess I was made to feel rather foolish by the generous-hearted extravagance of the tiny creatures.

Quite suddenly the shrill ovation came to a dead stop. For a moment I was puzzled. Applause does not naturally end thus; it dies down. Then I heard what sharp elfin ears had detected before mine—steps in the passage approaching the card-room.

The door was opened by a club steward. He strode across the room, and drew up the blinds, flooding the untidy room with intense sunlight. Only then did he notice me. He showed, and then suppressed, surprise.

"Beg pardon, sir," he said. "Have you been here all night?"

"Yes," I replied. Then I added brightly: "Good morning."

"Good morning, sir. I suppose you fell asleep."

I looked down at the table by which I was sitting. The cards were spread out on it in the four hands I had been analysing just before my strange adventure began. But now all four Sevens were the right way up.

I smiled at the steward.

"No," I told him. "I have not been asleep."

DEVYN PRESS INC.

3600 Chamberlain Lane, Suite 230, Louisville, KY 40241

1-800-274-2221

CALL TOLL FREE IN THE U.S. & CANADA
TO ORDER OR TO REQUEST OUR 64 PAGE
FULL COLOR CATALOG OF BRIDGE BOOKS,
SUPPLIES AND GIFTS.

DEVYN PRESS INC.
3600 Chamberlain Lane, Suite 230, Louisville, KY 40241
1-800-274-2221
CALL TOLL FREE IN THE U.S. & CANADA
TO ORDER OR TO REQUEST OUR 64 PAGE
FULL COLOR CATALOG OF BRIDGE BOOKS,
SUPPLIES AND GIFTS.

Lawrence & Hanson WINNING BRIDGE INTANGIBLES .... $ 4.95
Lipkin INVITATION TO ANNIHILATION .... $ 8.95
Michaels & Cohen 4-3-2-1 MANUAL .... $ 2.95
Penick BEGINNING BRIDGE COMPLETE .... $ 8.95
Penick BEGINNING BRIDGE QUIZZES .... $ 6.95
Powell TICKETS TO THE DEVIL .... $ 5.95
Reese & Hoffman PLAY IT AGAIN, SAM .... $ 7.95
Rosenkranz
    BRIDGE: THE BIDDER'S GAME $12.95
    TIPS FOR TOPS .... $ 9.95
    MORE TIPS FOR TOPS .... $ 9.95
    TRUMP LEADS .... $ 7.95
    OUR MAN GODFREY $10.95
Rosenkranz & Alder BID TO WIN, PLAY FOR PLEASURE $11.95
Rosenkranz & Truscott BIDDING ON TARGET $10.95
Silverman
    ELEMENTARY BRIDGE FIVE CARD MAJOR STUDENT TEXT ...... $ 2.75
    INTERMEDIATE BRIDGE FIVE CARD MAJOR STUDENT TEXT .... $ 2.95
    ADVANCED & DUPLICATE BRIDGE STUDENT TEXT .... $ 2.95
    PLAY OF THE HAND AS DECLARER
    & DEFENDER STUDENT TEXT .... $ 2.95
Simon
    WHY YOU LOSE AT BRIDGE $11.95
Stewart & Baron
    THE BRIDGE BOOK, Vol. 1, Beginning .... $ 9.95
    THE BRIDGE BOOK, Vol. 2, Intermediate .... $ 9.95
    THE BRIDGE BOOK, Vol. 3, Advanced .... $ 9.95
    THE BRIDGE BOOK, Vol. 4, Defense .... $ 7.95
Thomas SHERLOCK HOLMES, BRIDGE DETECTIVE .... $ 9.95
Von Elsner
    THE ACE OF SPIES .... $ 5.95
    CRUISE BRIDGE .... $ 5.95
    EVERYTHING JAKE WITH ME .... $ 5.95
    THE BEST OF JAKE WINKMAN .... $ 5.95
    THE JAKE OF HEARTS .... $ 5.95
    THE JAKE OF DIAMONDS .... $ 5.95
Woolsey
    MATCHPOINTS $11.95
    MODERN DEFENSIVE SIGNALLING .... $ 4.95
    PARTNERSHIP DEFENSE .... $ 9.95
World Bridge Federation APPEALS COMMITTEE DECISIONS
    from the 1994 NEC WORLD CHAMPIONSHIPS .... $ 9.95